Interrupting Cycles of Early Loss, Trauma and Abuse

This volume offers rich and detailed illustrations of the complex emotional needs of the children and parents in vulnerable families. The chapters also highlight the psychological toll that working with at risk groups takes on therapists and others charged with providing care for children and families whose internal worlds are often fragile and external worlds are often dangerous and chaotic. Above all, the contributions, whether taken together or individually make it abundantly clear that short-term solutions are simply not possible for adults or children who have been traumatized many times over. They also underscore the need for those working with traumatized groups to protect themselves from psychological exhaustion in order to maintain the emotional vitality that is necessary for effective work.

This book was originally published as a special issue of the *Journal of Infant, Child and Adolescent Psychotherapy*.

Toni Heineman is a Clinical Psychologist with over 30 years of experience working with children, adults, and families. She is the Founder and Executive Director of A Home Within, a national organization dedicated to meeting the emotional needs of current and former foster youth through relationship-based therapy and practices.

Interrupting Cycles of Early Loss, Trauma and Abuse

Therapeutic Challenges

Edited by
Toni Heineman

Routledge
Taylor & Francis Group
LONDON AND NEW YORK

First published in paperback 2024

First published 2014
by Routledge
4 Park Square, Milton Park, Abingdon, Oxon, OX14 4RN, UK

and by Routledge
605 Third Avenue, New York, NY 10158

Routledge is an imprint of the Taylor & Francis Group, an informa business

British Library Cataloguing in Publication Data
A catalogue record for this book is available from the British Library

Publisher's Note
The publisher accepts responsibility for any inconsistencies that may have arisen during the conversion of this book from journal articles to book chapters, namely the possible inclusion of journal terminology.

Disclaimer
Every effort has been made to contact copyright holders for their permission to reprint material in this book. The publishers would be grateful to hear from any copyright holder who is not here acknowledged and will undertake to rectify any errors or omissions in future editions of this book.

ISBN: 978-1-138-78047-7 (hbk)
ISBN: 978-1-03-293087-9 (pbk)
ISBN: 978-1-315-77042-0 (ebk)

DOI: 10.4324/9781315770420

Typeset in Garamond
by Taylor & Francis Books

Contents

Citation Information

The chapters in this book were originally published in the *Journal of Infant, Child and Adolescent Psychotherapy*, volume 11, issue 4 (December 2012). When citing this material, please use the original page numbering for each article, as follows:

Chapter 1
Introduction
Toni Heineman
Journal of Infant, Child and Adolescent Psychotherapy, volume 11, issue 4 (December 2012) pp. 297–298

Chapter 2
"Terrible Twos" and "Terrible Teens": The Importance of Play
Joan Raphael-Leff
Journal of Infant, Child and Adolescent Psychotherapy, volume 11, issue 4 (December 2012) pp. 299–315

Chapter 3
Containment, Trauma and Coherence: A Case Presentation and Discussion
Marian Birch and Quen Zorrah
Journal of Infant, Child and Adolescent Psychotherapy, volume 11, issue 4 (December 2012) pp. 316–341

Chapter 4
The "Dead Mother Syndrome" and the Child in Care: A Framework for Reflecting on Why Some Children Experience Multiple Placement Breakdowns
Carolyn Hart
Journal of Infant, Child and Adolescent Psychotherapy, volume 11, issue 4 (December 2012) pp. 342–355

Chapter 5
When the Lullaby is Missing: Healing from an Infancy in Foster Care
Amy L. Cooper
Journal of Infant, Child and Adolescent Psychotherapy, volume 11, issue 4 (December 2012) pp. 356–367

Chapter 6
Relationship Violence and Teenage Parents
Ambra Born
Journal of Infant, Child and Adolescent Psychotherapy, volume 11, issue 4 (December 2012) pp. 368–375

Chapter 7
Fostering Healthy Attachment Between Substance Dependent Parents and Their Infant Children
June Madsen Clausen, Rosana M. Aguilar and Mark E. Ludwig
Journal of Infant, Child and Adolescent Psychotherapy, volume 11, issue 4 (December 2012) pp. 376–386

Chapter 8
Fostering Relationships with Children Who are "Too Much to Handle"
Saralyn Ruff and Julia Baron
Journal of Infant, Child and Adolescent Psychotherapy, volume 11, issue 4 (December 2012) pp. 387–399

Please direct any queries you may have about the citations to clsuk.permissions@cengage.com

Notes on Contributors

Rosana M. Aguilar is the Lab Manager for the Foster Care Research Group at the University of San Francisco, USA. Rosana also works as a Family Support Specialist at a local non-profit organization that provides developmental screening and home-based early childhood mental health services for children 0–5 years of age and their at-risk caregivers.

Julia Baron is the former Referral Coordinator for A Home Within. A native San Franciscan with a BA from Colgate University in New York, Julia is a student in the PsyD program at The Wright Institute in Berkeley, California, USA.

Marian Birch, DMH, is a Clinical Psychologist and infant mental health specialist. She has practiced, taught and written extensively about infant-parent psychotherapy with severely traumatized families. She is a member of the Clinical Faculty of the Barnard Center for Infant Mental Health and Development at the University of Washington, USA.

Ambra Born, PsyD, is Director of Child Psychological Services for Reaching HOPE. She also serves as the Clinical Director of the Denver branch of A Home Within and Chair of the Board of Directors for How to Read Your Baby.

June Madsen Clausen, PhD, is Chair and Professor of Psychology at the University of San Francisco in San Francisco, California, USA. Dr. Clausen teaches undergraduate clinical courses, directs the Foster Care Research Group, and maintains a clinical practice in which she treats survivors of trauma.

Amy L. Cooper, MA, MFT, is a Psychotherapist and Qigong Teacher. She has advanced training and expertise in both Sensorimotor Psychotherapy for the treatment of trauma and Infant-Parent Mental Health and has presented nationally and internationally on trauma informed practice.

Carolyn Hart is Principal Child and Adolescent Psychotherapist in Sheffield, UK, where she works in a state-funded, specialist team for looked-after children. She initially trained in psychodynamic psychotherapy for children and adolescents at the Tavistock Clinic London. She is interested in creating bridges between relational theory and British object relation theory.

Toni Heineman, LCSW, DMH is a Clinical Psychologist practicing in San Francisco for over thirty years. She works with children and adults and divorcing families. Dr. Heineman is the Founder and Executive Director of A Home Within, a national non-profit organiation that offers pro-bono mental health services to current and former foster children. She is the author of *The Abused Child: Psychodynamic Understanding and Treatment* and Co-Editor of *Building A Home Within: Meeting the Emotional Needs of Children and Youth in Foster Care*, and *Treating Trauma: Relationship-Based Psychotherapy for Children, Adolescents, and Young Adults.* She has presented to a wide range of audiences and published extensively on the emotional lives of children and families.

Mark E. Ludwig, MSW, is Graduate Faculty Instructor in Somatic Psychology at the California Institute of Integral Studies, California, USA. He co-leads the Fostering Mindful Attachment intervention with his colleague, Amy L. Cooper, MFT, and maintains an adult, child, and infant-parent private practice in Berkeley, California.

Joan Raphael-Leff, PhD, is a Psychoanalyst and Social Psychologist specializing in reproductive and early parenting issues, with more than 100 peer-reviewed publications and 11 books published in this field. She led the Teen-Parenting Project at the Anna Freud Centre in London and is Honorary Professor at UCL, the University of Essex, UK, and Stellenbosch University in South Africa.

Saralyn Ruff is Associate Director of Research at A Home Within and Assistant Professor in the Psychology Department at the University of San Francisco. She is a Clinician with experience in community counselling and private practice, and a Co-Editor of *Treating Trauma: Relationship-Based Psychotherapy for Children, Adolescents, and Young Adults.*

Quen Zorrah, RN, MSN, Infant Mental Health Specialist, has worked in Public Health for 20 years offering home visits to families with young children, pregnant women, grandparents, foster parents, and fathers as primary caregivers. She completed the Certificate in Infant Mental Health at the University of Washington, USA, in 2003 and has integrated infant mental health into home visiting. She is currently the Nurse Consultant for Washington State Nurse-Family Partnership.

Introduction

Toni Heineman

I am honored to have the opportunity to bring the articles in this special issue of the *Journal of Infant, Child, and Adolescent Psychotherapy* to the attention of our readers. Each article offers a rich and detailed picture of the complex emotional needs of one or more vulnerable populations. The articles also highlight the psychological toll that working with at risk groups takes on therapists and others charged with providing care for children and families whose internal worlds are often fragile and external worlds are often dangerous and chaotic.

The children and parents we meet in this volume come to treatment with a multitude of challenges that are not easily understood or addressed. Yet in the current economic and therapeutic climate, those in the mental health fields are often expected to produce quick and measurable results with very limited resources. Too often, those with the least training are asked to do the hardest work with the least amount of support.

The articles in this volume, whether considered individually or together, make it abundantly clear that quick fixes simply are not possible for adults or children who have been traumatized—frequently many times over. They also underscore the need for those working with traumatized groups to protect themselves from psychological exhaustion in order to maintain the emotional vitality that is necessary for effective work.

The first article in the volume was a keynote address at the Nurturing Parents Conference held in Denver, Colorado, in October 2011. "'Terrible Twos' and 'Terrible Teens,'" by Joan Raphael-Leff, brings a developmental lens to the world of teen parents and their children.

"Containment, Trauma, and Coherence," by Marian Birch and Quen Zorrah, was the keynote address at the May 2011 Conference of the Washington Chapter of the World Association of Infant Mental Health. The authors walk us through the almost paralyzingly painful family treatment following the infant's being brutally abused by his father.

As the title indicates, "The 'Dead Mother Syndrome' and the Child in Care: A Framework for Reflecting on Why Some Children Experience Multiple Placement Breakdowns," by Carolyn Hart, explores the psychological contributions to the frequent moves many children suffer in foster care.

"When the Lullaby is Missing: Healing from an Infancy in Foster Care" by Amy L. Cooper describes the integration of the practice of QiGong into a psychodynamic treatment of a young teenager who spent her infancy on the streets with her homeless mother followed by a series of abusive foster homes.

The special issues facing teen mothers who are entwined with physically and sexually abusive partners is the subject of "Relationship Violence and Teenage Parents" by Ambra Born.

"Fostering Healthy Attachment Between Substance Dependent Parents and Their Infant Children," by June Madsen Clausen, Rosana M. Aguilar, and Mark E. Ludwig, discusses the outcomes of a program based on infant massage.

Finally, "Fostering Relationships with Children Who are 'Too Much to Handle,'" by Saralyn Ruff and Julia Baron, introduces a web-based program for staff working with pregnant and parenting teens and youth transitioning from the foster care system.

In every article, we are reminded how easily those with few emotional resources or external supports can become disregulated and what a profoundly deleterious effect that can have on all aspects of their lives. These articles also stress the importance of allowing ourselves to truly know the horrors that so many disenfranchised populations face on a daily basis, including those who receive few monetary, social, or psychological rewards for working with traumatized populations. The temptation to look away, minimize, or rationalize the pain of chronic trauma can be overwhelming. I hope that the articles in this volume will help us all remember that engaging our minds is one of the ways that we individually and together can stay psychically alive and able to continue to work in almost impossible situations.

"Terrible Twos" and "Terrible Teens": The Importance of Play

Joan Raphael-Leff

In the process of individuation, toddlers and their adolescent parents share similar dynamics; that is, both are involved with anxiety-laden preoccupations about difference and separateness and about bodily changes, loss of control, and containing aggression. Both experience internal struggles between emotional vulnerability and a sense of invincibility; both make fierce self-assertive bids coupled with a powerful need for guidance. When synchronized, such teen-toddler similarities can create a bond of mutual excitement; when their intentions clash, however, a terrible battle of wills erupts, fuelled by furious frustration or intense despair.

It is suggested that play can provide an essential bridge between teen parent and toddler, enabling each to work through his/her anxieties and passionate reactions of love and hate. Joint play increases reciprocal understanding. However, a teen deprived of play in childhood, or one who resents her/his own playtime being curtailed by parenthood, may become intrusive or controlling, projecting disowned aspects of her/his self into their mutual play. The parent thus breaks the play frame, creating confusion in the child between pretence and reality.

By providing a safe space to explore conflictual feelings through joint play, thoughtful practitioners can foster better emotional awareness and mentalization in troubled young parents and their toddlers.

The crucial issue in parenting is how to survive having life and death responsibility for the development of an incomprehensible vulnerable baby who turns into a defiant risk-taking toddler. I argue that this challenge is exacerbated for teenage parents, since they, like their children, are still engaged in developmental processes — some of which powerfully recapitulate issues first encountered during their own toddlerhood.

This paper addresses developmental parallels between toddlers and teens, exploring some aspects of clashes, conflicts, and co-operation between them. By presenting both perspectives, it aims to enhance emotional understanding in practitioners who work with this high-risk group.

At this time of rapid change, both toddler and teen undergo massive physical and emotional changes, alternating between use of more primitive and sophisticated areas of the brain. In addition, like the toddler, the teenager vacillates between dependency needs and desired autonomy.

This conflict manifests in blunders and tantrums when infantile processes intrude into reasoned decision making. It also shows up in rebellious altercations with authority figures over limits and rules. Both teen and toddler experience internal struggles between emotional vulnerability and a sense of invincibility, fearing loss of control and uncontained aggression. For many teenaged parents, previous defences prove inadequate to cope with the toddler's escalating demands and their own pressing internal issues, resulting in terrible emotionally charged battles.

I suggest that playfulness offers a way of reducing tension, to restore contact between warring young parent and toddler. While play enables each to work through his/her own intense issues and passionate experiences of love and hate, it also increases awareness of the other's feelings. Imaginative play also serves a variety of crucial functions for both teen and toddler's developing minds, learning to manage their respective anxieties and practicing confrontations in relative safety. Pretend role-reversal facilitates better understanding of each other and fosters mentalization in both teen and toddler. However, for some adolescents, play itself feels dangerous, liable to arouse unresolved feelings, especially when previous defenses prove inadequate to cope with the rapid evocations of past, present, and future internal and external issues.

The emotional effects of such failed defences are amplified when a child is involved. Parents who are preoccupied with their own issues will find it hard to mirror a child's emotions without engaging their own. Unable to reflect or to have fun, they resort to controlling, intrusive, or dissociated behaviors while playing with the toddler.

CHANNELING DESIRE

For both toddler and teen we may distinguish between an early period of false belief that s/he can be and do anything and a sobering time of discovering *limitations*. For the toddler, the painful experience of having to renounce previous unrealistic omnipotence and oedipal longings is made tolerable by the promise of someday becoming big and powerful, finding a mate outside the family, and having a baby of his/her own. These relinquished desires are re-examined again in the light of bodily changes in puberty. Loss of the comparative safety of childhood brings new gains: when an adolescent becomes sexually active the old oedipal triangle is rotated and rather than excluded, s/he is now one of an erotic couple. The new combination of fertility and greater physical strength is a heady yet frightening experience — having the *actual* power to seduce, conceive, destroy, or even kill. No longer just in fantasy, now a real possibility, it dictates new responsibilities.

For some teens, this new power heightens awareness of the potential consequences of their actions, instigating a greater sense of body ownership and self-restraint. Others, for a variety of nonconscious reasons, get caught up in competitive rivalry, reckless physical excitement, or escapist activities, using their bodies to externalize their own internal conflicts and desires.

Adolescence can be an alarming time for young people who, fluctuating between intensely upbeat and despondent emotions, sometimes fear that they are going mad. In vulnerable teens, reawakened conflicts thus lead to intensified risk-taking activities. Escapist solutions are common and may consist of eating disorders (e.g., anorexia, compulsive binging, bulimia), abuse of alcohol, and other addictive substances; compulsive masturbation, excessive exercise, social isolation, or disproportionate Internet use; sexual promiscuity, self-mutilation or dramatic suicidal bids, tyrannical or delinquent tendencies, or violence toward others.

In girls, such activities often reflect difficulties in differentiating from the same-sex mother. Cutting or self-burning may be a disguised attack on the maternal body or on the changed pubertal body. Similarly, premature motherhood can be seen as a message to the mother: an unconscious communication of neediness or competitiveness. Pregnancy can also alleviate a pubertal girl's anxiety about losing her mother's care. Refinding maternal support with her baby reassures her that she has not killed or damaged her mother by usurping her (Laufer, 1996). Sometimes, pregnancy may seem to offer a way of bypassing adolescence and refusing its challenges.

However, many of these escapist manifestations are now so commonplace among Western teenagers that practitioners regard them as a social trend rather than recognizing external expressions of depression, persecutory disorders, anxiety states, or posttraumatic stress disorder (PTSD) following childhood insecurity, deprivation, or abuse.

GENDER AND GENERATIVITY

During adolescence, salient issues of identity, gender, and sexual desire take on new meanings as childhood appetites and fantasies undergo a further round of reappraisal. Western societies allocate a prolonged period for exploration and modification of these expectations before assigning young people to adult commitments and responsibilities. However, for reasons of their own, some teens choose to speed up generational succession by becoming parents themselves.

Gender formation is a lifelong process that begins in toddlerhood, emerging dialectically through primary relationships, and physical, psychic, and socio-cultural experience. To become a mature adult, a teenager must re-evaluate the four constituents of gender which s/he first negotiated as a toddler. I define these as *"gendered embodiment," "role representation," "eroticism,"* and *"generative agency"* (Raphael-Leff, 2007). For most adolescents, the last of these, *generative agency* (the sense of self as a potential creator), takes the form of sublimated activity, that is, engagement in intellectual or creative pursuits (music, art, film, craft hobbies, school work, games, sports or leisure projects). For others, the subcultural gender-code may dictate quite drastic, often irreversible acts, involving tattoos, body piercings, self-harm, forbidden substances, risk-taking bravado, or gang cultures of crime or violence. Yet others seek self-worth in *procreation.* To them, the ultimate enticing outlet is to create not a substitute but rather a *real* baby as did the originary parents. While accidental conceptions do occur, choice of teen parenthood is not randomly determined.

Empirical studies find a five-fold rate of earlier sexual activity and teenage conceptions among girls whose fathers left the family during the daughters' childhoods (Ellis et al., 2011). When fathers have been peripheral or absent, girls often treat their male peers with considerable contempt, turning to older men, who themselves suffering from lack of self-esteem and inadequate role models, privilege sexual conquest above intimate relationships (Waddell, 2009). In fatherless girls and those unaccustomed to tenderness, a man's jealous possessiveness and even aggression may be interpreted as caring ("He loves me such much he goes ballistic if another boy even speaks to me". . .). Many young people who were fostered or grew up in children's homes find a biological connection through childbearing. Seeking the family they wish they had had, there is a disproportionate representation of youth leaving the care system among those having babies precipitously. Finally, the propensity to enact conflicts that cannot be symbolized impels some teenagers to choose parenthood as a means of bypassing the emotional work of adolescence.

Needless to say, reasons for conceiving are multidimensional, involving conscious design and unconscious motivations, including

- Dicing with fate: magical denial of consequences of unprotected sex; romanticizing an accidental pregnancy;
- Wanting to prove fertility (rather than desire for a baby);
- Low self-esteem: a search for identity, a purpose in life;
- Aspiring to become fully adult/to emulate mother or father;
- Loneliness, disillusionment, or a response to social rejection;
- Needing someone to love and/or someone to be loved by;
- Succumbing to peer or subcultural social pressures;
- A last-ditch attempt to save a failing relationship;
- Hoping to get out of home, or to create a new home;
- Conveying an unconscious message of triumph, need, or despair to one's own parents;
- A desire to flesh out a fantasy baby;
- Wishing to recapture lost aspects of one's own babyhood;
- Wanting to repair or renegotiate incomplete developmental tasks;
- A fantasy of creating the perfect family/rewriting history;
- Cheating death (especially if faced with life-threatening circumstances or bereavement).

TRIALS OF TEEN PARENTING

In general, Western societies grant adolescents an experimental phase of preparation for adulthood. Premature parenthood inevitably deprives a teenager of time to gradually process and resolve the conflictual feelings commonly experienced during adolescence. Furthermore, caring for a baby churns up intense emotions. Thrust into meeting the infant's needs, the teenaged mother or father finds his/her own preverbal experience powerfully evoked, stretching internal (as well as external) resources to the limit. When the infant becomes a toddler parental depletion is further exacerbated by competition between the child's omnipotent wish for self-sufficiency ("by'm'self") and the teen-carer's need to feel competent, assertive, authoritative, and obeyed.

Inevitably, for both toddler and adolescent, the journey toward greater emotional awareness and physical self-reliance involves anxiety-provoking challenges. In common, teen parent and child are both experiencing massive bodily and social changes which activate their concerns about normality and belonging. Both are preoccupied with experiences of birth, death, and sexuality and with the need to negotiate difference and separateness. Each in his/her own way is very much engaged with finding out about emotions — understanding the feelings of others and their own intense experiences of love and hate, how to contain aggressive feelings and to channel sexual urges.

However, these similarities are asymmetrically loaded: the teen parent has an ethical duty to protect and nurture the more vulnerable child in her/his care.

Intuitively, most carers of young infants speak a form of motherese, that is, a high pitched, repetitive, rhythmic form of baby talk. They spontaneously match the child's prevailing emotional mood and then tend to mirror it. What is interesting is that they do so in an *exaggerated* way, thereby providing social biofeedback, which gradually enables the growing child to recognize his/her own emotions and to differentiate these from the carer's feelings, which are not so overstated (Gergley & Watson, 1996). However, where parental emotion is overloaded and too similar to the child's (as happens with adolescents), the baby may feel confused as to whose emotions are being expressed in the mirroring. This is crucial because by reflecting and naming feelings, a parent not only cultivates the child's emotional literacy about his/her own feelings but also sharpens awareness of the mental states that guide human behavior in *others*.

Young carers may be unable to mentalize (think about) their child's emotions. Feeling bitter about being stuck at home when their peers are out enjoying themselves yet also deprived of time alone, they resent the toddler's rowdiness and feel intensely irritated by what appear to be incessant demands for attention. Picky eating, sleep disturbances, regressive incontinence, and anxious clinging all further enrage the young parent who had glimpsed freedom once the baby began to walk.

When she does get a chance to get out, in her wish to escape a young mother may brush aside the child who clings to her, trying to prevent her departure by screaming furiously and clutching at her legs. Seeking her reassurance, the toddler clings harder as the teen mother desperately tries to get away, tersely overlooking the child's urgent need to restore a sense of security. Conversely, if she has some regular respite, separations become a benign reality for both and a means of self-replenishment.

By contrast, control over the growing child's body, intake, and growth may reflect a mother's wish to remain the main source of resources as she was during pregnancy and early infancy. Such control may be an expression of other feelings as well. A fashion-conscious teen mother may focus on controlling choice of clothing, treating the child as a doll to be dressed or an accessory, feeling that her son or daughter's inappropriate apparel will reflect badly on her own taste and appearance. Battles ensue if the child's feelings and need to own his/her own body is ignored. For teen-toddler dynamics are such that as the odds stack up, mutual demands to be consulted escalate into a screaming match, which a more experienced mother may have avoided. Lacking a partner with whom to debrief, a single mother who is the sole target of tantrums and defiant testing is more vulnerable to attack, and may not have the time, patience, or emotional resources to acknowledge the toddler's frustration without hitting back verbally or physically.

In addition, teenage mothers are often isolated, deprived of the company of their school-attending friends, whose carefree leisure activities she misses as childcare takes precedence. Her resentment may spill over into the relationship with her child.

Mothering is a three-generational process involving the young mother's past experience of being mothered (Pines, 1988). The present relationship to her baby and sexual partner are affected by internal representations of her mother, herself, and her unconscious fantasies, expectations, and wishes. When negative aspects of these remain unresolved with the birth of her child they involve a submissive attitude to hide aggressive feelings in her ongoing struggles to differentiate herself from her mother. The teen's baby daughter may feel disempowered by her young mother's lack of agency. On becoming a toddler, the little girl may feel that her own wish for separation-individuation will damage her same-sex carer. This may dovetail with the feelings of the teen mother, who feels jilted and abandoned by the child who chooses to explore rather than stay close by her, which in turn increases the child's guilt and insecurity. This intricate conflict of interests is especially intense when a young mother who, like all adolescents, is still individuating herself and uncertain about her own separate identity, feels unsure of the difference between firm self-assertiveness and aggression.

Similarly, lacking confidence in her own entitlement to achieve, a young mother may hand over her ambitions to the child, fostering inflated uncritical expectations. Or fearing aspects of her own exuberance, she may severely control these in her toddler's behavior, or conversely might subtly encourage rather than restrain socially unacceptable rambunctiousness.

JUBILATION

Why is toddlerhood the critical time? When sometime near the first birthday, the infant undergoes a momentous change, the dramatic transition from crawling to standing marks a major milestone within the family. To the caregivers, the upright infant seems to double in size overnight. To the child, standing offers a different perspective of on all she/he surveys, and a speedy mode of locomotion, an exhilarating hands-free experience for tool using and far-reaching investigation. Imitating the parent's activities facilitates a sense of similarity to m/other. Exploration increases the sense of separateness. The young toddler also becomes increasingly inventive, capable of making new linguistic combinations, and playing with old toys in innovative ways.

A "love affair with the world" (Greenacre, 1957) ensues as the inquisitive toddler finds *everything* exciting and develops new bodily capacities such as walking, trotting, and eventually climbing, jumping, running, and even skipping. Bodily control and a sense of influence over the environment are extremely pleasurable, especially when this enjoyment is reflected back by an appreciative loving carer. As initial unsteadiness rapidly gives way to walking, the young toddler takes pleasure in bodily sensations and skills — forever experimenting and taking spills and accidents in his/her stride. Daringly, the child extends boundaries of her/his personal world, finding new places, new objects, new words, new activities and capacities. But s/he also wants to *share* this newfound excitement, inviting interaction by using more gestures and some words. Jubilant, delighted, and proud of his/her physical powers, the newly mobile child is always on the lookout for adventure but needs approval.

However, exploration often leads to forbidden activities and places and unmitigated exuberance provokes anxiety in carers as the young child cannot fully anticipate the dangerous consequences of actions. Researchers estimate that previously permissive parents now issue a prohibition to the 11–17 month old approximately every nine minutes (Schore, 1994). Having felt joyously all-powerful, at a year and a half s/he is confronted with both environmental constraints and his or her own limitations. The child responds by eagerly sharing special objects in the hope of generating reciprocity and encouragement to make further, perhaps joint, discoveries.

However, the sense of invincibility now wears thin. By combined clinging and intentionally aggressive behaviours towards the caregiver the toddler tries to defend two seemingly irreconcilable fronts — the need for *agency* and for *attachment.* Anxious about capitulating into passive surrender yet afraid of losing the carer's love (Freud, 1952), the toddler struggles with contradictory internal impulses and restrictive external realities, becoming emotionally volatile and outraged by encroachments that challenge his/her illusion of magical control (Stoker, 2005; Zaphiriou Woods & Pretorius, 2010). How this is met by the carer will influence the child's self-confidence and security.

TERRIBLE TIMES

During toddlerhood babble becomes differentiated into increasingly recognizable words. The infant's delight in producing sounds is replaced by a new urgency to communicate and to be understood. Young parents who have struggled to understand a preverbal baby hope to find this stage easier now that the young child can articulate his/her needs. But the child's frustration increases as vocabulary lags behind thinking. There is so much that cannot be expressed without responsive help from the carer. A young father who feels stymied by the toddler's seemingly irrational panic over a torn bit of paper or adamant refusal of a broken cookie might respond differently if he grasped the child's anxiety about irreversible damage or fear of being abandoned.

From around 20 months, clashes escalate between the toddler's desire for unlimited exploration and the parental wish to impose safety restrictions or socially acceptable habits. A fifteen fold increase occurs in the carer's use of verbal admonitions (*"Don't do that!! I said NO!"*). If healthy curiosity predominates over injunctions, the toddler will persist, keen to investigate novelty, differences, and similarities.

Disobedience becomes an issue, and a busy parent may interpret the child's wish to climb up and walk along every low wall or visit every front garden on the way home as willful dawdling or intrusion rather than inquisitiveness. Carers may resent the child's never-ending questions and feel persecuted by his/her need to know everything. Some feel controlled by the child's invasion of the parental bed.

Unbridled experimentation with physical objects also extends to body exploration. Researching bodily boundaries and sexual difference, toddlers take delight in their nakedness, locating, exploring, and finding names for their genitals, and pleasurable feeling while exploring orifices — behaviors that vulnerable young parents may find challenging. If the teen has unresolved issues around sex and sexuality, these confrontations are likely to be particularly fierce.

Toddlerhood also heightens awareness of bodily functions such as tiredness and energy, wounds and healing, hunger and satiation, digestive peristalsis, physical experiences of pleasure and pain, and a deep interest in controlling or relinquishing bodily substances, including burps, farts, pee, and poop. For some parents, experiences of incontinence, refusal to bathe, and tactile interest in feces increases their disgust. They mistrust the unpredictable nature of control over bodily sphincters, feeling the child is doing it on purpose. This poses essential questions about body management.

Toddlers are now discovering the power of aggression — biting, hitting, and temper tantrums which often result in intense confrontations. The child makes a frantic bid for body *ownership,* resisting any encroachments. S/he rejects enforced toilet training and insists on choosing books, clothes, and food and the sequence of events. Help is resisted, and the child throws a mighty wobbly when his/her style is cramped. These reactions, in turn, often goad the young caregiver into wanting to *"show who's boss,"* and a battle of wills ensues.

Recognition of separateness heralds a cognitive change in the young toddler. Awareness of different physical perspectives is demonstrated by the new capacity to follow the carer's gaze, rather than finger, when something is pointed out (Hobson, 2002). This revolutionary change indicates perception of *intersubjectivity,* meaning that the child who up to now has felt her/himself to be the center of the world gradually begins to realize that s/he is merely part of it and that others are subjects with feelings of their own, which may be different from his/her own.

The urge for unrestricted exploration now begins to vie with anxiety about angering the parent. To avoid this prospect, the toddler interacts more avidly. S/he tries to placate the mother or father, bringing small peace offerings and seeking affirmation and comfort when tired, hungry, lonely, or uncertain.

However, like the young child outraged by restrictions, the young carer, too, craves self-determination. Parental self-sacrifice clashes with ordinary adolescent desire for carefree play time. Continuous obligations weigh heavily. When a teen parent's defenses fail during these fraught encounters, his/her own troubled childhood experiences are revived and unconsciously transmitted to be absorbed by the perplexed child.

As the growing child acquires better understanding of the subtleties of interpersonal signals, s/he is puzzled and distressed by admonitions. A growing sense of justice questions seeming unfairness — why others withhold things and forbid access yet demand sharing — reprimanding him/her for hoarding toys, or possessively referring to all objects as mine. Timing is an issue — toddlers want to have everything — and they want it now. But busy carers need time. Melt downs occur when the impulsive child is told to wait despite a burning desire for immediate gratification.

While younger toddlers manifested their distress in eating and sleep disturbances and crying, older toddlers tend toward extended displays of negativism and defiant disobedience. In the latter stage of the *terrible twos* (which sometimes extends into the threes) mood swings, impulsive actions, and awesome temper displays occur, paralleled only by the terrible inner turmoil of screaming door-slamming, obnoxious young teenagers.

Parental ascriptions proliferate at this time. Mothers with abusive partners may attribute the child's age-appropriate rambunctiousness as malevolent or out-of-control aggression, originating in the violent father (Lieberman, 1999). Normal acquisitiveness may be treated as greed, sexual curiosity regarded as perverted, inquisitive exploration misinterpreted as ransacking, or legitimate anger as sadism. Shamed in public by the uncontrollable toddler and feeling outmanoeuvred and disobeyed, the embarrassed teenaged parent may resort to scathing sarcasm or physical violence to stop the toddler from rampaging in the shopping mall. However, a slap to halt the tantrum endangers the young parent's self-respect, and provides neither understanding nor appropriate anger management for the child.

Before an infant is able to preserve a stable positive representation of the mother in her absence, s/he experiences intense feelings of love and hate, splitting off the idealized carer from the hated one. However, as in all fairy stories, the witch and the good fairy are different facets of a single figure. Gradual recognition that the split loved/hated good/bad caregiver is one and the same person has two effects. The toddler's mixed feelings become more integrated but also accompanied by regrets about his/her attacks and fear of losing the carer's affection (Klein, 1952). The shame, guilt, and anxiety involved in this realization can feel devastating to the toddler. The parent's tolerance helps develop compassion and appreciation that others have their own emotional needs and, hence, subjective reasons for their responses. A growing ability to see things from different viewpoints enhances the toddler's empathy as well as recognition of the other's liability to judge.

The terrible era thus rages on both sides of the teen-toddler frontier, peaking when feelings of uncontainable anger, confusion, hurt, and frustration predominate. As noted, some toddler behaviors, such as eating bogeys or taking pleasure in wetting, soiling, smelling, and playing with turds and/or open masturbation, may arouse disgust and uncontained fury in puritanical teens. Such repugnant manners are especially disturbing to the defense-dominated adolescent parent who is still in the throes of suppressing his/her own primitive aspects. Put to the test, s/he may feel deeply ashamed following aggressive outbursts, including cruel teasing, physical harshness, or actual violence. The young parent may recognize the irony of being unable to control his/her own raw feelings while demanding that the toddler also do so.

Under pressure, an exasperated teen finds it hard to mentalize and consider connections between his/her own disproportionate rage and the child's naughty behavior. In turn, sensitive toddlers tend to respond to inconsistent handling with increased disorganization, but the teen parent may not see the child's accident proneness as a need for comfort. Yet antisocial activities and/or hurting themselves may seem the only outlet for emotionally abused children to express their distress. The confused child may retaliate with aggression while begging for forgiveness or resort to defensive measures of lying, hiding persistently, or running away.

The terrible period is difficult for any parent to manage. However, it is especially so for adolescent parents who themselves are simultaneously reworking of many of these same emotional issues. Their own unresolved history, unformed personality, and difficult external circumstances make them extremely vulnerable to "*contagious arousal,*" reflecting the turbulent feelings and fantasies their toddler evokes in them. Exposure to unprocessed nonverbal emotions and direct contact with primal substances (such as amniotic fluid, lochia, breast milk, urine, and baby feces) re-activates nonsymbolic experiences, thus increasing paternal as well as maternal susceptibility to postnatal emotional disturbance (Raphael-Leff, 1991, 2012).

ATTACHMENT AND EMOTIONAL REFUELING

Finally, the toddler's capacity to walk, and indeed to walk *away*, heightens concerns about getting lost and losing. Able to venture quite far, the animated 2-year-old may suddenly freeze midstride feeling overwhelmed by separation anxiety. S/he needs frequent emotional "refueling" (Mahler, Pine, & Bergman, 1975). Under duress, we all experience the need for protective care. Teenage parents themselves also still yearn for security and emotional refueling from their own attachment figures in order to provide care for their child.

Attachment theory states that to feel secure enough meet the world confidently, a child needs both easy access to the carer and encouragement to experiment further (Lieberman, 1993). Inevitably, anxieties are increased when the primary caregiver leaves for work, or the child is dropped off at day care. These anxieties manifest in sleep disturbance and bad dreams by night, and contradictions by day — clinging and darting away, hitting out and wanting to be comforted, demanding to be consulted yet carried or fed like a baby.

However, it is important to distinguish between ordinary conflicts of toddlerhood and more severe disturbances. When a good experience has been internalised, it provides the toddler with a core of security that can be drawn upon in the carer's absence. Indeed, availability of this internalized secure base determines the radius of the child's freedom to explore the world. It is directly related to the *quality* of his/her attachment (Bowlby, 1988). One's life-long experience of self-confidence comes from learning to manage sadness, anger, and anxieties in a safe context with responsive carer who survives without collapsing, retaliating, or attacking (Winnicott, 1971).

When distressed, a securely attached toddler seeks contact and feels comforted by the carer who holds him/her in mind. However, if a carer is dismissive of the child's emotions, and is controlling, intrusive, rejecting, or neglectful, the insecurely attached toddler will become *avoidant* — cultivating a pseudo-independent stance by defensively deactivating her/his need for emotional attachment. When a teen parent is inconsistently enmeshed and withdrawn, the toddler will exhibit features of insecure *anxious* attachment, heightened vigilance and little spontaneous exploration in his/her presence. On the other hand, some parents are emotionally unavailable because they are overly preoccupied with their own unresolved emotional issues. Their toddlers manifest *disorganized* patterns of attachment with disoriented behaviors such as freezing and approach-avoidance. When a mother or father also unconsciously enacts past experiences of trauma or loss, the trapped child may resort to extreme forms of escape — head-banging or dissociation in relation to the carer's frightening or abusive responses.

Through cumulative experience, each toddler evolves an inner representation of his/her primary attachment figures, an Internal Working Model (IWM) that forms an *expectation* of future relationships (Bowlby, 1969) and, unless processed consciously, persists throughout life as a template. Thus, romantic relationships of adolescents are also shaped by their own early attachments, with secure teens developing a higher quality of connection based on their own caregivers' perceptions of love (Roisman et al., 2005). Insecure parents tend to repeat the unsatisfactory, neglectful, or even abusive relations they had with their own carers.

Finally, practitioners too are guided by their own internal working models. Some find it difficult to work with teenage clients because of the degree of anxiety involved and the keen ability of adolescents to pit one professional against another, which increases the tendency for splitting within diverse and multiagency teams. In addition, a worker's own unresolved feelings about adolescence are factors. A manualized training has been devised to help a variety of practitioners in their work with teen parents and their children. Enhanced understanding occurs not only about the typical emotional states, psychodynamic processes, and developmental issues of teen parents and their offspring but also of institutional and personal dynamics (Raphael-Leff, 2012).

CLASHES, CONFLICTS AND CO-OPERATION

A child who is well-supported and securely attached finds ways to self-soothe and keep bodily states under control. In infants, this self-regulation may take the form of thumb sucking or fondling a special toy or security blanket. In time, a child who has been consistently helped to understand can begin to self-reflect and process his/her own emotions. Ideally, at the same time, *interactive regulation* occurs, with growing mutual understanding and reciprocal coordination of inner and relational processes increasing the child's sense of influential agency. Conversely, an unsupported toddler who has had to self-regulate prematurely may become blocked-in, applying rigid tactics to manage arousal states.

Throughout this article it is stressed that emotional experiences with primary caregivers are important in shaping the toddler's emerging sense of self. Parental containment modulates and "down-regulates" painful affect, especially when parents themselves are not too aroused by the child's distress. However, parents who are unable to monitor and modify their own negative feelings also have difficulty modulating the child's levels of affect when these are too high. Interaction with a stressed carer actually *creates* stress, leaving the child with an intrusion of undifferentiated chaotic feelings, embedded in subsymbolic states of mind. Recent research suggests that *stimulus overload* (where carers allow experience to exceed the baby's threshold barrier) can cause long-lasting changes in the immune system.

Lack of containment is a major source of disturbance in infants during the first year, resulting in frequent and enduring high levels of negative affect and little pleasure. The baby remains distressed for longer and displays excessive crying, feeding difficulties, and sleep problems. This in turn may aggravate the situation by engendering parental hostility and a sense of being duped or emotionally exploited (*"She just does that to annoy me."*) Teenagers are particularly susceptible to the negative effects of disrupted sleep, which hinder their ability to cope with daily stresses.

Clearly, the child's defenses, such as hypervigilance or dissociation, are strategies to avoid unmanageable affects and ward off unpredictable intrusions. Mothers and fathers also have habitual defenses which derive from threats in their own childhoods. These are activated in present situations, especially where they cannot tolerate seeing their own disavowed anxieties reflected in the child. But the tendency to reject similar feelings in themselves makes them unreliable mirrors for their infants. When misattunement is a chronic situation, the baby neither learns to identify her/his own feelings nor develops a smooth transition between emotional states. S/he exists in a state of *hyperarousal* with deficits in self-regulation. Insensitively raised toddlers have difficulty organizing and modulating their own emotional states. Chronic deprivation and unpredictable, disrupted care generates states of *contin*ual intense arousal — overactivity associated with attention deficit hyperactivity disorder, overvigilance, anxiety and panic disorders, depression, eating disorders, addictions, and borderline personalities in later life.

We have seen how the toddler's bids for autonomy echo the adolescent's struggles over control, separateness, independence, and competence. How these are co-handled is crucial, as it is during late toddlerhood that identifications are consolidated for better or worse.

Toward the end of toddlerhood, a *"why phase"* signifies the young child's determination to identify patterns and learn how the shared world works. Instruction around *behavioral control* becomes ever more significant to the senior toddler who is trying to learn social regulations. When told what to do, while still resisting, even the child who fiercely negates suggestions will also try to emulate the carer. If the urgency of prohibitions was previously ignored, the growing child now both defiantly refuses them, yet makes a personal attempt to control his/her own behavior. When confronted by an enticing stimulus, the child reiterates the parental "no!", often retracts his/her arms behind the back, or waggles a finger to resist temptation. Where previously a toddler used social referencing, that is, checking the carer's face to see whether something was safe, acceptable or repulsive, s/he now asks questions. In some families, rules are clarified, and what is permitted or forbidden is spelled out and explained. In others, the rationale remains unfathomable as "goal posts" shift inconsistently. Concerned to understand and comply with social systems, the older child expands boundaries by imitating peers and elders. Parents, who are aware of the child's growing capacity for reason and self-regulation, shift their expectations. No longer demanding instant compliance, they try to negotiate a compromise based on explanation, appealing to common sense about not doing acrobatics on a chair, cutting his/her own hair, or poking toothpicks through the butter. The combination of loving encouragement and increased competence help the child toward more realistic self-esteem and a sense of satisfaction in his/her newfound physical, mental, and social capacities.

During this third year, as principles are abstracted and taken in, an *internal conscience* is consolidated. Obedience is no longer dependent on the carer's presence. The child learns to monitor his/her own behavior and eventually to take responsibility for affect regulation, exerting control over modes of expression their carers and peer group deem inappropriate.

SELF–REGULATION

Young parents tend to enjoy the child's growing command of communicative language. Their freedom grows in parallel to the little girl or boy's ability to tolerate separations, failure, and frustration. Simultaneously, for this very reason, they feel even more provoked by occasional crankiness, negativism, and blatant refusal to collaborate.

The area of ambivalence is particularly difficult for teens whose struggle with their own mixed feelings was disrupted by parenthood. An immature mother or father may find it impossible to survive a child's verbal attacks without collapsing into guilt, convinced s/he has failed and is being judged and rejected. Conversely, s/he may become angry, vindictive, and retaliatory.

Of necessity, parents must impose constraints to minimize risk and to restrain the growing child's defensive omnipotence and desire for boundless exploration. However, this is not easy for a teenager who personally feels unable to apply restraint. Attempts to instill a sense of social niceties backfire when the teen yells at the child to "ask nicely" rather than demand. Many a young parent still needs firm limit-setting, coupled with warmth and support, from her/his own parents. Finding it difficult to provide age-appropriate boundaries, the teen may inconsistently overstate control and then abandon regulation altogether, thereby increasing the child's sense of omnipotence, confused withdrawal, or defiant rebellion. Furthermore, an adolescent's emotional lability gets in the way of establishing social restrictions and safe boundaries. If this has not abated, their own impulsive need for immediate gratification obstructs attempts to teach the child to wait. Indeed, a savvy toddler may reverse roles, reprimanding the parent for shouting, smoking, littering, or drinking too much. Thus, identification with carers (of either sex) helps the child to hold on to the carer internally. However, if the internalized figure is felt to be hostile, critical, or domineering inside, the child may become clingy, needing constant external reassurance and benign acceptance to modify the cruel controls s/he has set up within (A. Freud, 1981).

The problems of boundary setting often result in the adolescent capitulating or losing self-control. Parental episodes of aggressive teasing, physical harshness, violence, and/or emotional retaliation escalate the level of the toddler's negativism. Indifference to abuse or apparent lack of concern about the consequences of antisocial behavior indicate hardening defenses. Other thinly disguised expressions of distress are accident proneness, masochistic manifestations, or anxious overcompliance.

On the other hand, when a carer continues to be empathically responsive to the child's contradictory needs without mockery, rage, or retaliation, this affirms their basic trustworthiness. The trusting child establishes an internal image of a "good-enough" carer (Winnicott, 1971) who has faith in the child and holds him/her in mind. This also allows the child to trust in his own capacities. Overcoming separation anxiety, s/he can now spend longer times apart and at greater distances away from the "secure base" (Bowlby, 1988), attending day care or nursery.

The challenge of responding to contradictory declarations of adoration and intense hatred is most disconcerting to a teen whose motivation for early parenthood was a craving for love. Like the child, the adolescent is also intensely engaged with heightened aggression and eroticism as well as notions of age and gender inequalities. It is here that play become so essential.

PLAY

The importance of play cannot be overestimated. Mutual play can form an essential bridge between toddler and teen parent. A fun situation which facilitates mutual understanding, it may also be seen as a "precursor for adult work" (A. Freud, 1981) and a prime means of developing new skills of communication and social functioning. Through numerous role-play activities, the child builds up a sense of unique individuality reinforcing an increasingly multifaceted identity and more complex view of the important people in his/her life. As the distinction between objective and subjective realities becomes clearer, pretend modes of play replace the uneasiness of psychic equivalence when the child assumed the realism of his/her fantasy and its omnipotent projection into the world (Fonagy & Target, 1996).

Playing together has inestimable benefits in developing understanding and empathy between toddler and teen. Play offers both participants a *safe arena* for reformulating their anxiety-provoking experiences. By playing out a variety of roles, including each other's (*"Now you be the baby and I'm the daddy"*), new compassion is generated between parent and child, enabling them to better see each other's viewpoint and appreciate their respective difficulties.

Through enjoyable playtime together, both toddler and teen can explore what the other feels and thinks, can master their own anxieties, and use fantasy to compensate for their own painful frustrations. However, teen parents who have missed out on play in their own childhoods or those who currently feel deprived of their own leisure play time may resent providing a happy experience for their child. Play may start well, but they find themselves taking possession of the best toys or enviously spoiling the child's game. A carer who is unable to play or one who feels threatened by the emotions it arouses may detach her/himself while playing. S/he may control the risky side of play by steering the topic away from dangerous subjects or overdirect imaginary scenarios. A troubled parent may dissociate or become remote in the course of play. Another may be too intrusive, directing the child's narrative or inserting his/her own script. When the carers project their own disowned feelings into the play space, it distorts the play experience by breaking the safe frame of pretence, thus creating anxiety and confusion between fantasy play and reality.

Attending a play group can open up new horizons for both parent and child. Seeing the way other teen-toddler pairs play can help a parent to set limits or verbalize the child's fears and wishes (see Zaphiriou Woods & Pretorius, 2010). Playing within a group situation also increases the child's understanding of rules of social procedures, allowing a safe space to practice extremes and to modify expression of sexuality and aggressiveness in socially acceptable ways, thus reinforcing the process of socialization. Through play with friends the toddler develops pride in learning new activities and will want to rehearse and exhibit these at home (often at most inconvenient times).

During the period of late toddlerhood, language rapidly becomes more sophisticated. Play expands the child's vocabulary in size, richness, and complexity, in tandem with increasing awareness of the emotional intricacy of self and others. The growing child who previously used his or her name as signifier now says "I" and "me," as rudimentary symbolic thought gives way to logical structures, with a growing capacity for humor, and play becomes more elaborately imaginative. Soaring beyond restrictions through imaginative play the child learns to negotiate both the illusion of his/her omnipotence and its realistic limitations.

Around age 4, integration of different modes of functioning occurs when the child begins to perceive thoughts and feelings as *representations*, and is more capable of reflecting upon these

(Fonagy & Target, 1996, p. 470). Body ownership and impulse control are also consolidated over the fourth year, with completion of toilet training and mastery of skills such as drawing people, lacing beads, skipping, hopping, galloping, and bike riding. Additionally, by converting the imaginary into imaginative play, the inner world is populated and the limits of experience expand. With a growing sense of ownership, the child who recognizes that others cannot read his/her private thoughts is now capable of keeping a secret or lying with ease.

In general, playing with new permutations of self-other representations alleviates anxiety. Playing with impossible ideas provides a new sense of agency as innovations promote greater confidence and a sense of pleasure and power forming a springboard to further creativity (Raphael-Leff, 2010). Many teen-toddler conflicts can be negotiated through solitary or mutual play, which is multifunctional and can be used to

- process anxiety-provoking situations and complex ideas;
- compensate for painful frustrations;
- plan ahead, practice and rehearse new possibilities;
- reformulate impulses in a socially acceptable way;
- reinforce a sense of cultural belonging;
- cultivate a plurality of experiences through alternative conceptual narratives and roles;
- develop inventiveness by fostering a variety of new combinations;
- recognize and actualize internal facets in the external world.

Above all, for teen parents, pretend role reversals and empathic listening in play can enhance their reflective function and capacity to mentalize.

MENTALIZING WITH TODDLERS

Parental reflective function pivots on an ability to change perspectives and to see the child's needs as *separate* from their own. The capacity to mentalize, that is, to bear in mind the other's desires, intentions, and anxieties, depends on an ability to think about feelings without becoming overwhelmed by the child's or one's own unintegrated anxiety or hostility (Fonagy, Gergely, Jurist, & Target, 2002). Although as capable as anyone of doing this, a self-conscious adolescent parent may feel embarrassed in public or too preoccupied with his/her own similar or discrepant feelings to have the mental space to consider the toddler's feelings separately.

An unruffled carer soothes the distressed child rather than causing further disruption. However, mothers or fathers who are unable to reflect on their own feelings become easily dysregulated themselves. When they become disorganized by the child's expressions of pain or rage, what they reflect back fails to distinguish between their own feelings and those of the anxious child. An overinvolved carer becomes alarmed and guilt-ridden, unable to step back and think about possible reasons for the toddler's negative feelings, rather than feeling overwhelmed by these. A teenager who feels criticized or rejected by the child and/or persecuted by parenthood may become irritated, intrusive, and frightening, which further bewilders the child.

Ideally, parental mentalization includes dual *self-reflective* and *interpersonal* components (Fonagy et al., 2002), which enable both carer and child to distinguish inner from outer reality, pretend crying, or provocative teasing from "real" suffering or defiance. The ability to make these subtle distinctions is especially important when parents feel exposed and tested to their limits by intensely negative emotional displays, such as the toddler rampaging in the supermarket while adults look on disapprovingly at both mother and child.

If *"I hate you!"* is treated as a declaration of war rather than a cry of frustration and becomes a focal point rather than seen as one aspect of the toddler's jumble of mixed feelings, the parent's hostile reaction may actually give her/him cause to be hated. Furthermore, when a carer is unable to disentangle their own feelings from the child's tangle, s/he unconsciously projects their own repudiated impulses into the toddler who then becomes the carrier of false ascriptions (e.g., a monster, a weakling, a greedy guts) and unconsciously internalizes these unwanted attributions as part of the self.

BRAIN AND MIND

We know that adolescents are capable of empathy and interested in feelings. However, in their self-centered preoccupation, they tend to be less aware/responsively aroused to the needs of others. In fact, when tested, younger mothers do not show the same patterns of increased heart rate and cortisol in response to a baby's cries that older mothers do. Some researchers attribute this diminished attunement to adolescent neural immaturity while the medial prefrontal cortex (the brain region important for planning and executive functioning) is still developing (Giardino, Gonzalez, Steiner, & Fleming, 2008).

Neuro-scientific studies show that, like the rapid growth in the prefrontal area that occurs during toddlerhood, the pubertal brain also undergoes a further wave of reorganization. At this time, toddler and teen are both undergoing massive brain changes, and both of them alternate between use of more primitive and sophisticated areas of the brain. The young mother or father may consciously try to do things differently, but while embroiled in a state of adolescent "storm and stress" s/he unwittingly continues to operate from implicit feelings. These are "programmed" by his/her own archaic carer's deficiencies and, in turn, molds the brain of the child in her/his care. ("I had sworn I'd never say that! I sound just like my Dad!") We now know that not only the child's personality but his/her very *brain circuits are shaped and pruned by caregiving patterns* (Balbernie, 2001). During this critical early period of prolonged dependence, the baby's endowment is activated, modified, or inhibited by the specific carers with whom s/he interacts. Studies find that emotionally damaging effects of the caregiver's depression, abuse, or neglect are associated with permanent maladaptive neural response patterns in the child, affecting neurobiological stress systems (Pollock, 2005; Watts-English et al., 2006). This has long-lasting results. For instance, a meta-analysis of 16 studies (23,544 participants) found that childhood maltreatment more than doubles the risk of persistent depression in adulthood (Nanni, Uher, & Danese, 2011).

In sum, human nature is multifaceted. Many developmental features that appear to be driven purely by a built-in genetic program or by conscious parental design are the result of a complex interplay of cross-generationally embedded as well as embodied and environmental elements.

CONCLUSION

We have seen that the dynamics of a toddler's passionate self-assertion coupled with powerful internal struggles are not unlike those of the young adolescent fiercely upholding the right to be different and independent. Both are involved with playing-out contradictory impulses of love, hate, sexuality, age-appropriate claims to body-ownership, anxieties about loss of love, separation, and merger. When the toddler's carer is a teenager the similarity of their emotional experience creates a bond of mutual excitement. Yet teens and toddlers are set on paths that may challenge and antagonise each other. Clashing goals provoke reactions of fury or despair if their respective wills are thwarted and the child's intense feelings contagiously arouse equally intense responses in a teenage parent, who has not yet resolved these concerns about limitations and control.

It is difficult for a young mother or father to maintain their cool in the face of their toddler's ambivalence, despite realizing that their angry response and controlling behavior raise the toddler's anxieties about his/her and the carers' destructive powers. Humor and play offer a safe arena in which such conjoint preoccupations can be played out and explored by both. The carer's readiness to play and to repair the relationship following their inevitable clashes reinforces the toddler's belief in being lovable and understood. Through ongoing pretend playful exchanges and especially role-reversal games, both can explore their concerns and begin to understand the nature of the other's feelings and reasoning.

Some teenage parents are lucky enough to benefit from engagement with a thoughtful practitioner who can render the child's infuriating behaviors understandable and more tolerable. Practitioners themselves can be more understanding when they see how the toddler's highly charged bid for autonomy enrages the young parent because s/he too craves independence, and it also undermines her/his fragile sense of authority. By reflectively mitigating some of the teen's blind spots, the sensitive practitioner can further the capacity for self-regulation in both parent and child.

In order to mature within their living systemic relationship, *both* toddler and teen need to be recognized and to recognize the other as having a similar yet separate mind. This involves acknowledging their sameness but also their *difference* — different capacities, different age-determined needs, and different perspectives on their shared world. However, due to their asymmetry, the adolescent parent also has an obligation to guide the child and to acknowledge and repair their misunderstandings. Simultaneously, through identification with a receptive thoughtful carer, the child's capacity for reflectiveness is enhanced. When feelings are treated as significant, the toddler is motivated to be considerate to others and to take responsibility for his/her own. Importantly, the experience of successfully parenting a toddler offers the teen a growth opportunity — a second chance to recognise and work through his/her own conflictual emotions and to evolve an increasingly complex coherent sense of self alongside the child's doing so.

REFERENCES

Balbernie, R. (2001). Circuits and circumstances: The neurobiological consequences of early relationship experiences and how they shape later behaviour. *Journal of Child Psychotherapy*, *27*, 237–255.

Bowlby, J. (1969). *Attachment: Attachment and loss (vol. 1)*. London, England: Hogarth Press.

Bowlby, J. (1988). *A secure base*. New York, NY: Basic Books.

Ellis, B. J., Bates, J. E., Dodge, K. A., Fergusson, D. M., & Horwood, L. J. (2011). Does father absence place daughters at special risk for early sexual activity and teenage pregnancy? *Child Development*, *74*, 801–821.

Fonagy, P., & Target, M. (1996). Playing with reality: I. Theory of mind and the normal development of psychic reality. *International Journal of Psychoanalysis*, *77*, 217–233.

Fonagy, P., Gergely, G., Jurist, E., & Target, M. (2002). *Affect regulation, mentalization, and the development of the self*. New York, NY: Other Press.

Freud, A. (1952). A connection between the states of negativism and of emotional surrender. *International Journal of Psychoanalysis*, *33*, 265.

Freud, A. (1981). The concept of developmental lines: Their diagnostic significance. *Psychoanalytic Study of the Child*, *36*, 129–136.

Gergely, G., & Watson, J. S. (1996). The social biofeedback theory of parental affect-mirroring. *International Journal of Psychoanalysis*, *77*, 1181–1212.

Giardino, J., Gonzalez, A., Steiner, M., & Fleming, A. S. (2008). Effects of motherhood on physiological and subjective responses to infant cries in teenage mothers: A comparison with non-mothers and adult mothers. *Hormones & Behavior*, *53*, 149–158.

Greenacre, P. (1957). The childhood of the artist. *Psychoanalytic Study of the Child*, *12*, 47–72.

Hobson, P. (2002). *The cradle of thought: Exploring the origins of thinking*. London, England: Macmillan.

Klein, M. (1952). Some theoretical conclusions regarding the emotional life of the infant. In *Envy and gratitude and other works, 1946–1963* (pp. 61–93). London, England: Hogarth Press.

Laufer, M. E. (1996). The role of passivity in the relationship to the body during adolescence. *Psychoanalytic Study of the Child*, *51*, 348–364.

Lieberman, A. F. (1993). *The emotional life of the toddler*. New York, NY: The Free Press.

Lieberman, A. F. (1999). Negative maternal attributions: Effects on toddlers' sense of self. *Psychoanalytic Inquiry*, *19*, 737–756.

Mahler, M. S., Pine, F., & Bergman, A. (1975). *The psychological birth of the human infant*. New York, NY: Basic Books.

Nanni, V., Uher, R., & Danese, A. (2012). Childhood maltreatment predicts unfavorable course of illness and treatment outcome in depression: A meta-analysis. *American Journal of Psychiatry*, *169*, 141–151.

Pines, D. (1988). Adolescent pregnancy and motherhood: A psycho-analytical perspective. *Psychoanalytic Inquiry*, *8*, 234–251.

Pollock, S. D. (2005). Early adversity and mechanisms of plasticity: Integrating affective neuroscience with developmental approaches to psychopathology. *Development & Psychopathology*, *17*, 735–752.

Raphael-Leff, J. (1991). *Psychological processes of childbearing*. London, England: Chapman & Hall.

Raphael-Leff, J. (2007). Femininity and its unconscious 'shadows': Gender and generative identity in the age of biotechnology. *British Journal of Psychotherapy*, *23*, 497–515.

Raphael-Leff, J. (2010). The 'dreamer' by daylight — imaginative play, creativity, and generative identity. *Psychoanalytic Study of the Child*, *64*, 14–53.

Raphael-Leff, J. (2012). *Working with teenage parents*. London, England: The Anna Freud Centre.

Roisman, G. I., Collins, W. A., Sroufe, L. A., & Egeland, B. (2005). Predictors of young adults' representations of and behavior in their current romantic relationship: Prospective tests of the prototype hypothesis. *Attachment and Human Development*, *7*, 105–121.

Schore, A. N. (1994). *Affect regulation and the origin of the self: The neurobiology of emotional development*. Hillsdale, NJ: Erlbaum.

Stoker, J. (2005). *You and your toddler*. London, England: Karnac.

Waddell, M. (2009). Why teenagers have babies. *Infant Observation*, *12*, 271–281.

Watts-English, T., Fortson, B. L., Gibler, N., Hooper, S. R., & De Bellis, M. D. (2006). The psychobiology of maltreatment in childhood. *Journal of Social Issues*, *62*, 717–736.

Winnicott, D. W. (1971). *Playing and reality*. London, England: Tavistock.

Zaphiriou Woods, M., & Pretorius, I. M. (2010). *Parents and toddlers in groups: A psychoanalytic developmental approach*. London, England: Routledge.

Containment, Trauma and Coherence: A Case Presentation and Discussion

Marian Birch
Quen Zorrah

Very challenging cases require containment on many levels. This paper illustrates just such a coordinated, multilevel response to a complex treatment situation. Infant mental health specialist Quen Zorrah, RN, MSN, describes her relationship-focused work over 18 months of infant-parent psychotherapy, advocacy, and systems management in a case involving parents and their severely battered infant. Because a reflective individual and group consultation offered essential containment for the therapist, the consultant, Marian Birch, DMH, offers her thoughts on how both individual and the group consultation helped metabolize multiple anxieties and ultimately assisted the therapist, the parents, and community service providers to better respond to the child's physical and emotional trauma.

Warning: The following paper contains material that is or should be profoundly disturbing.

We will be discussing our work with a severely battered toddler, whom we will call Casey. Casey was 8 months old when he was airlifted to the regional trauma center with a severe head injury. Both of his parents ascribed his injuries to "a fall." He was injured at home with his father while his mother was at work. At first, his parents said he had fallen off a couch while his father's back was turned. Later, they said he had somehow fallen out of his father's arms and landed on his head. Whatever the true course of events, when he arrived at the hospital he was having seizures and had bilateral brain hemorrhages. There was evidence of an earlier, healing fracture of his radius, and a previous brain hemorrhage. The medical staff found Casey's injuries to be consistent with having been shaken, rather than falling.

As the title of our paper indicates, we will use Casey's case to address the interwoven relationships between "containment, coherence and trauma." We ask you to pause in the narrative at this point and close your eyes for a moment. Observe your internal state in response to this description of Casey. It is probable that you are either feeling quite stirred up or have already engaged your preferred modes of managing arousal in order to stay calm. Despite our long familiarity with this story, we found that while writing this paper we had to constantly recheck our notes because, on some level, we wanted so much to forget, to not know what happened to Casey.

We are discussing events that happened several years ago, to someone whom none of our readers have ever met or seen, yet as they read our story most of them will be contending with subjective states of arousal that have the evolutionary function of preparing us to fight, flee from, or escape the notice of tigers. Casey's story will call upon the reader not only to think about containment but also to practice it.

When we have presented this story in person, at this point we have led our listeners through a breathing exercise, one that activates the parasympathetic nervous system and deactivates the sympathetic nervous system by slowing down and lengthening the rate of the breath, and by extending the length of the exhalation relative to the inhalation. Listeners have let us know that doing this exercise helped them to be more aware of their own internal somatic and visceral responses to the subsequent presentation. For those who would like to try this, directions are in an appendix at the end of the paper.

Perhaps the reader, like the authors, has had the frustrating experience of presenting hard-won ideas about deeply troubling — even traumatic — material, only to find that audiences become so distressed by the story that they can neither think about the presenter's ideas nor generate coherent responses of their own. Instead, audience responses often feel designed to be reassuring, to help us all go on not knowing and not feeling what is so distressing to know and feel. It is extremely difficult to remain calm and coherent while also allowing oneself to feel the experience of a traumatized infant. One has to constantly pull back from the Scylla of disorganization or the Charbydis of dissociation. We are not sure that this can be altogether avoided, but we ask you to try to stay aware of what the material touches in you and to think about if and how you find the mental balance that allows you to know about extremely difficult, primal mental states without being undone by them.

DEFINING TERMS: CONTAINMENT, COHERENCE AND TRAUMA

Each of these terms is widely and variably used in ordinary discourse and in the literature of psychotherapy. The definitions that follow are not meant to be definitive or comprehensive, merely to clarify the discussion that follows.

Containment involves procedures, applied to oneself or to another, that serve to help the one who is being contained to avoid the overwhelming experience of fear and danger and concomitant incoherent disorganization of self that characterizes traumatic states. Some examples of such containment procedures are holding, changing the physical environment, rocking, empathic mirroring, soothing, breathing deeply, listening intently, vocalizing and verbalizing, and mentalizing. Although containment is a noun, it is important to keep in mind that it is an active, dynamic process (Schafer, 1976).

Coherence is a state in an individual, dyad, or group characterized by balanced, flexible access to responses to the social and physical environment that are developmentally appropriate and integrated. Such integrated, adaptive responses include physiological, affective, cognitive, perceptual, sensory, proprioceptive, kinesthetic, and relational components.

Trauma is an overwhelming subjective experience of fear and danger, in excess of one's capacity for integrated, adaptive response. For our purposes, trauma is not an external event but rather an internal state of unmanageable, unbearable dystonic arousal. The subjective experience of trauma is the same in people of all ages and situations, but its precipitants can vary tremendously.

The brain, the nervous system, the emergent self, and the attachment behavioral system of the infant and young child are dynamically growing, organizing, and integrating at a breathtaking rate. Much of this development requires and incorporates the features of the caregiving environment. The young child has limited resources for self-regulation and needs containment by the caregiving environment in order to maintain or regain ongoing coherence despite the flood of internal and external change that characterizes development.

When the environment is unable to provide containment, this alone may be traumatizing for the infant who cannot yet self-regulate without support. The developmentally appropriate behavioral schemata for containment that are operational in an infant are limited. Those that the infant can use without help are very costly, for instance, numbing and dissociation. More adaptive schemata are attachment behaviors (such crying, reaching, gazing, and clinging) and the concomitant affective states that motivate and accompany them. By definition, these schemata are not effective without a responsive caregiver.

When the environment is actually a source of extreme fear, distress, and danger, words fail us as we attempt to describe the subjective state of the infant. Winnicott used the term "primitive agony" to characterize experiences that overwhelm the infant's unsupported adaptive capacities (Winnicott, 1963).

Containment, provided to the infant by her caregivers in their community, is critical to the infant's capacity to slowly organize a coherent sense of self in relationship with others. The infant's brain and nervous system are in an embryonic state. It is only when or if impingements are minimized by adequate parental care that the infant is able to learn and mature, acquiring increasingly sophisticated skills for self-containment and self-regulation. The learning that occurs in calm, alert states is far more nuanced and flexible than that which occurs in states of disorganized arousal.

Containment of an infant by a caregiver critically requires the caregiver to believe that the infant's behavior means something. The caregiver must also believe that s/he, with an older, wiser, more experienced brain, can know what that meaning is, can psychically digest that meaning, and can mirror it back in a way that gives the baby a subjective sense both of being understood and of understanding her own experience.

Without containment by a caregiver, an infant often has no framework to know what his internal feeling means, until this is communicated by his caregiver's actions, gestures and vocalizations. Containment is critical for the infant's emerging sense of connection and increasing sense of inner coherence (Fonagy et al., 2002).

To express this in the language of attachment theory, the primary function of the attachment relationship is to provide actual safety, while its secondary function is to provide the felt security necessary for optimal learning and growth. These are often, but not necessarily, co-occurring.

In the following case discussion, we will explore the interplay of containment, coherence, and trauma in our intervention on behalf of a profoundly traumatized infant. We will look at the interplay between containment, coherence and trauma at four levels:

- In the child, Casey, in the context of his familial environment,
- In Casey and his parents in the context of the community of family and institutions in which they live,
- In the intervening infant mental health therapist, Quen Zorrah (hereafter QZ), in the context of the professional context in which she worked. This includes the array of agencies, colleagues and educational and professional resources to which she had access,
- Finally, in the intervening infant mental health therapist, QZ and her consultant, Marian Birch (hereafter MB), as well as the consultation group in which they participated, during the course of Casey's treatment.

CASEY: PART I

Casey's expressive behavior, which QZ observed during his supervised visits with his parents and grandparents, in his foster home, and in his earliest interactions with her, told QZ the truth of his experience. However, this truth may not have existed in Casey's mind in any coherent and accessible way before QZ understood it and let him know what she understood. This truth, that he had been utterly dependent for survival on parents who actively threatened his life, was so painful and so frightening that QZ knew immediately that she would need support and containment herself in order to allow herself to know what she knew and in order to find the courage to voice what she knew to herself, to her support network, to Casey's parents, to protective services, and to the family court judge. In fall 2001, when QZ applied to the Certificate Program in Infant Mental Health at the University of Washington, she was working as a public health nurse in a rural county implementing David Olds' Nurse-Family Partnership curriculum (Olds et al., 1997). This program provides frequent home visits, case management, developmental guidance, and psychoeducation to high-risk families from the second trimester of pregnancy until the age of two. When MB, then Clinical Coordinator of the certificate program, asked QZ during her admission interview why she was applying, she replied, "Now that I'm spending so much time listening to these women, I feel like I don't know what to do with what they are telling me."

Ten years later there was a remarkable echo of this feeling of not knowing in the exchange below between QZ and Casey's mother, Daphne. QZ identified this exchange, captured on videotape, as "the moment where my attachment relationship with Daphne began." As Casey desperately and persistently tried to initiate physical closeness and snuggling, trying over and over to climb into her arms, Daphne sat on the floor, repeatedly redirecting him to the toys and away from her, saying plaintively, "I don't know how to hold my baby." Over those ten years of clinical experience doing home-based intervention with extremely high-risk families and receiving the collegial containment that the work required, QZ is now able to find words to describe not only what she should do or what she needs to do, but also words for what she actually does but cannot always see alone. At the time of referral, QZ was contracted with child protective services to provide parent-infant assessments and psychotherapy to families challenged with issues of abuse and neglect. MB had been her clinical consultant for ten years, and she had been part of a consultation group facilitated by MB with two other clinicians for five years. Each of these professional relationships placed an emphasis on supporting and normalizing the therapist's need for containment and support in order to work with traumatized and traumatizing clinical situations.

FROM REFERRAL THRU PRESENTATION OF FINDINGS TO PARENTS: QZ'S NARRATIVE

I first met Casey before his injury, when he was 6 months old. His mother, Daphne, brought him to the clinic where I worked when she came in to sign up for Women, Infants, and Children (WIC), a federal food assistance program for women with infants. I had plenty of time that day so I did his developmental screening. Daphne enjoyed trying new activities with Casey, and she readily answered my questions. We discovered that Casey was developing well in all areas. Daphne was very pleased with his accomplishments. She denied having any concerns about him. I remember finding Casey cute and lively as he crawled around the room playing with toys and feeling a little worried that he seemed too willing to crawl away from his mother in an unfamiliar room.

I next saw Casey two months later at the request of Child Protective Services (CPS). Two weeks earlier he had been discharged from the regional trauma center to foster care. I was asked to work with him and his parents during their supervised visits in the CPS office. I read Casey's medical file before our first visit. He had arrived at the trauma center by helicopter in critical condition, with a large bilateral brain hemorrhage. He was unconscious and having seizures. Although he had extensive hemorrhaging in both eyes and both ears, he did not have any bruises. A full body x-ray revealed that he had a partially healed fractured of his arm. His MRI showed a previous brain hemorrhage. The trauma specialists agreed that his injuries were consistent with abuse, specifically, with being shaken. The parents' accounts to the medical providers alleged an accidental fall, which did not match the medical findings.

Before I entered the visit room, I watched the family through the one-way mirror. Casey was in the visit room with his parents, Daphne and Ben, and two other adult relatives. The adults were talking animatedly together and seemed to be having a good time, almost as if they were at a party. There was a TV blaring and the room was brightly lit by overhead fluorescent lights. I watched as Casey, with a great deal of effort, slowly pulled himself across the floor to the toys. He was wearing a protective foam helmet. I knew that his brain was still bleeding and that he continued to have seizure activity. Just when he reached the toys, his father, Ben, abruptly picked him up without a word. Casey arched and made frantic movements away from his father. Without speaking or looking at him, Ben set him down on the floor at his feet and resumed talking to the other adults. Casey once more pulled himself laboriously to the toys. Again, just as he reached the toys, Ben picked him up. Again, Casey struggled silently and was returned to the floor. He was able to briefly get up on his hands and knees in a crawling position where he rocked back and forth, perhaps an effort at self-soothing. He trembled constantly. Casey remained totally silent through all this. He did not fuss or cry. He seemed both dazed and strangely pleasant.

With me in the tiny observation room, behind the one-way mirror, were the social worker, the visit supervisor, and the special advocate appointed by the court to represent Casey's interests. We were all getting more and more distressed as we watched. I grew increasingly alarmed by the disconnected chaos in the room. I was afraid that Casey was in imminent danger, both emotional and neurological. The other observing adults expressed their anxiety by pleading with me to go in the room and DO something. Their sense of urgency heightened my own.

As I knocked on the door of the visit room, I felt not just frightened but also angry. I was angry that Ben and Daphne were so blithely ignoring Casey's distress, angry that they caused his distress, angry that this baby had been so badly hurt. I was frightened by what appeared to be his imminent collapse into seizures or maybe a re-bleed in his brain. I was frightened by the knowledge that Ben was a violent and scary guy who had a criminal history of assault. The intensity of my feelings was amplified by my attunement to the disconnect between Casey's bizarrely cheerful facial expression and his increasingly frantic motor behavior. Somehow I contained any open expression of these feelings. I entered and introduced myself. I reminded Daphne that we had met a couple months ago. She smiled and cheerfully responded that she remembered me. Ben said the social worker told them that I would be coming to visits to help them.

Casey did not visibly respond to my entering the room. He was once again trying to pull himself to the toys. When I asked the parents how Casey's injury had affected him, Ben responded that his crawling was different. Daphne nodded and said he used to crawl up on his hands and knees and to move fast. We could all see that he was now dragging himself laboriously on his belly. Daphne was very cheerful as she told me this. At this point Ben picked Casey up. As he had each time his father had picked him up, Casey responded by arching, flailing, and trembling, all while avoiding eye contact with anyone. I struggled to appear calm; Casey's desperation was palpable and almost unbearable. I tried to keep my voice even and neutral as I told the parents that I thought Casey was in severe distress that put his brain in immediate danger. Probably, despite my efforts, my voice conveyed my sense of urgency when I stated that we had to do something about Casey's distress right now. Without waiting for Ben and Daphne to respond, I dimmed the lights, turned off the TV, and asked their relatives to leave. They started to argue with me, but they left. I started speaking in a very slow, very soft voice, almost whispering. I told Ben to turn Casey around so he was facing the center of the room. I showed him how to hold Casey firmly flexed with gentle pressure, a hold that is comforting and soothing to drug-affected newborns. In response, almost immediately, Casey became calmer. His muscles still trembled but much less. He started looking around the room, scanning rapidly, not focusing, and he continued to be eerily silent. Casey's face was fixed in an odd smile. I would come to know this expression as his "I'm not happy but I'm afraid to be upset" fake smile.

Returning my attention to his parents, I explained how the noise and lights were overwhelming his injured brain. Daphne then timidly asked Ben if she could hold Casey and he handed her the baby. Casey immediately turned his head away and pushed away from her. Once again taking control, I talked Daphne through holding him facing away from her and he calmed. Within minutes Ben took the baby from her. He did not say anything and Daphne did not protest. She did not attempt to hold Casey for the rest of the visit.

Speaking softly, I told them what I saw as Casey's experience of the visit. Daphne and Ben appeared interested in my description of how Casey might have felt earlier in the day when he was picked up by a stranger at his foster home, where he had been staying with strangers since his discharge from the hospital. He had then been strapped into an unfamiliar car seat, and brought into this unfamiliar room. All this strangeness was after being in a hospital where he had many strange people examining him and giving him shots while he was experiencing a great deal of pain and having seizures. I told them I thought that, in addition to the physical injuries to his brain, Casey was showing signs of posttraumatic stress disorder (PTSD). I explained what PTSD was and how it looked in an infant. Both parents seemed interested but oddly cheerful about this interpretation of Casey's experience, and they did not ask any questions. I expanded on what I imagined was Casey's experience, wondering if he felt frightened by them when they were loud and handled him abruptly.

As I talked, I observed that Casey was calming. He had no more tremors or flailing. He smiled and babbled a little at the room, being careful to avoid focusing on any person or object. I commented to Ben and Daphne that they had been successful in helping to reduce his stress. (Later in consultation group we wondered how Casey had experienced the presence of an adult who voiced what he felt. He would not have understood the words perhaps, but the contained but intense emotion they conveyed would have been palpable to an infant.) Ben, Daphne, and I spent a few quiet minutes watching Casey together. Then the visit supervisor came into the room to take him back to his foster home. Casey did not protest or show any affect during this transition. Neither did his parents mark the separation with any verbal or nonverbal expressions.

After he left us, I again narrated Casey's experience of the visit and of being with his parents. Both responded by telling me about their own distress. Daphne said only that she missed Ben's older son, a child she knew only from a few brief visits. I felt indignant at her striking disconnection from the emotional reality of her own child. Ben stated he was upset at being accused of hurting his son. He insisted that he would never hurt him and that he loved him very much. He said that Daphne's mother, Mary, who had often cared for Casey, was the one who hurt him. Ben started crying and told me he grew up in foster care and experienced severe abuse throughout his entire childhood. He said he really loved being a father, and his dream was to have a family. Although I noted and felt dismay at Ben's absorption in his own rather than his son's distress, I also felt a tug of empathy intruding into my anger at him. When Daphne became tearful, held his hand and looked lovingly at him, in marked contrast to her evident obliviousness to Casey's distress, I had to work to control my feelings of outrage. I suggested to Ben that he seek a psychological evaluation and therapy. He emphatically agreed that he needed and wanted help, but he asserted that no one would help him. I told him that their social worker would be offering mental health services as part of their family service plan and urged them both to participate. I wanted it to be clear that my help would be focused on Casey. As they left the visit room, they were cheerful and holding hands. I noticed that I felt sick to my stomach, repulsed, and disgusted. As I returned to my office I called MB to schedule a consult visit.

Then I sent a brief but strong statement to the social worker about the visit, including guidelines for keeping Casey safe during visits. I recommended having visits with only one parent at a time and stipulated that I could end a visit if the parents were not appropriate. I asked for the same visit supervisor for all transports and visits. I arranged for visits to be in the infant room, which had a rocking chair, sofa, and a few infant toys but no TV or noisy toys.

DISCUSSION

When we met for consultation a few days later, we reflected together on the extreme emotional virtuosity this intervention demanded. Briefly, the therapist needed simultaneously to:

- Attune affectively to a very traumatized, neurologically fragile and disorganized infant.
- Initiate a therapeutic alliance with the infant's parents, finding some way to empathize and be non-judgmental, to contain her responses of anger, revulsion and fear to their neglect and probable abuse of the baby.
- Find the edge of how much confrontation the parents could tolerate/bear/hear, in acknowledging the baby's distress and their responsibility for it.

- Maintain access to a detached, professional voice for communicating with the court and with medical providers effectively — in the language of observable, tangible, provable facts, not emotion
- Absorb and work with the intense and often unconscious emotional responses of other professionals and providers.

We noted that QZ had already taken charge. She had taken on the role of she-who-knows-and-must-be-obeyed both with the parents and the social worker in response to the sense of chaos and terror she felt in the visit room. We wondered how Casey had experienced her very active yet controlled management style.

QZ NARRATIVE RESUMED

A week later, I met the maternal grandparents for their first visit with Casey since his injury. Before he was hurt, they had cared for Casey in their home while Daphne worked. (On the day of the injury, Daphne had, unusually, left him home alone with Ben.) I introduced myself and explained that I would be joining their visit to guide them in understanding and responding to Casey's needs. When the visit supervisor carried Casey into the lobby, he immediately brightened. He made eye contact with each of them and babbled to them. He reached out to his grandmother, Mary. As she held him, he snuggled into her joyously. During their half hour visit Casey showed only brief distress. There was no trembling, no frantic movements or arching, and he consistently sought both body contact and eye contact with his grandparents. Mary was sensitive to his cues and responsive to my coaching. When she handed Casey his favorite stuffed animal, he hugged it happily.

Casey's visit with his mother was scheduled right after the grandparents. I asked Mary to stay for the first few minutes after Daphne's arrival. Mary held Casey as Daphne came into the visit room. Casey's affect immediately became flat. He did not look at Daphne or reach for her. He showed no interest in her at all. This was very distressing to watch, as I had just seen him demonstrate his capacity for remembering and relating. I had a brief moment of wondering if I was imagining all this.

When Mary left the room, Casey did not mark her departure and showed no distress at all. Daphne held him briefly and then set him down on the floor with a few toys, and she sat on the sofa. Casey sat still. He showed no interest in the toys. At my suggestion, Daphne joined him on the floor and showed him how to play with a toy. He glanced briefly at her but did not approach. Daphne kept cheerfully talking and smiling at him, acting oblivious that he was ignoring her. After a few uncomfortable minutes of watching this, I sat on the floor beside them and quietly joined the play. Casey did not look at me but scooted himself over to me until his back was touching my leg. Then he looked at his mother and started to play with her. I felt in awe of his capacity to find me and to believe that I could ground him as he tried to find his mother. Again, I fleetingly wondered if this was all in my imagination. I continued to coach Daphne quietly. They played together for about 10 minutes before Casey started to fuss. As his distress intensified, Daphne waved toys in front of him more vigorously and more quickly. I quietly coaxed her to pick him up, saying that he needed her to comfort him. I dimmed the lights as she picked him up. She was tentative and awkward but slowly she started to rock him and sing quietly. Casey slowly relaxed into her arms and turned toward her so that he could see her face. He reached up and touched her face and mouth, gazing into her eyes. I was quiet, holding my breath; their finding each other was so beautiful and felt so fragile, like a bubble that could easily burst. As I watched, Daphne said quietly, "I don't know how to hold him, how to care for him, Ben is much better at this than me." In my mind I recalled the way Ben always took charge with Casey, how he took the baby away from Daphne when she tried to hold him. My heart went out to her for the first time, transcending the anger and frustration I felt about her failure to protect and comfort her baby. I said softly and firmly that she did know how to hold her baby: that I could see her caring for Casey, that I could see she was holding him just right, and I could see him responding to her. I told her that these were important, healthy attachment behaviors. I wanted to contradict her belief in her failure, to protect her, to tell her that there was hope. This was my attachment moment to her. I suddenly felt that I would find the stamina to work with her. I wondered at the power of the serious emotional abuse she must be enduring, so insidious that she could not see her own baby in her arms.

DISCUSSION

When our consultation group watched the videos of this session and one from the same time period with Ben, we were all powerfully affected by how fragile and lost Casey appeared, his pale sober little face framed by his protective helmet, his movements painfully slow and arduous, and by how completely out of sync, even oblivious both parents seemed to be to his distress, even when his signals could not have been clearer to us. Part of what gave QZ the stamina to continue was the role her consultants played in tempering the desperate hope and longing to rescue that being with such a needy and lost infant stimulates in most adults. We told her repeatedly that we expected that this treatment would fail, that the parents' self-preoccupation and inability to see how hurt their son was made it doubtful they could form a therapeutic alliance with her on his behalf. We encouraged her to frame her efforts to make such an alliance, as part of what, initially, would be a forensic evaluation for protective services. In other words, she might be in a position, as an infant mental health expert, to explain to the court why this little boy should NOT be reunified with his parents. This permission to fail, this positive construction of what failure might accomplish, freed QZ to try her hardest to help, without unrealistic hope.

Consultation with other professionals who are experienced in work with extreme, primitive, and disorganized emotional states is vital to such work. It serves to validate the clinician's experience and relieve the common feeling that one's perceptions are crazy. Without it, the clinician's mind tends to try to resolve the extreme discomfort and radical disconnect between successive emotional observations by reframing crazy observations so that they make sense and by using detachment, dissociation, or distraction. It may take a village to see madness without becoming mad oneself. Perhaps this is analogous to how the raw, turbulent emotions of their infants may disorganize the minds of lonely and isolated new mothers.

QZ NARRATIVE RESUMED

Over the next three weeks, with the support of my consultation group and my individual conversations with MB, I framed what I was doing with Casey and his family as an extended, in-depth assessment. This helped me to hold at bay my own pervasive and persistent sense of an urgent need to DO something. It also served to contain the urgency and pressure coming in my direction from the family and from protective services. I used both the Diagnostic Classification 0-3 (DC 0-3, 2005) assessment guidelines and the Functional Emotional Assessment Scales (Greenspan & Weider, 2000) to organize my observations. I felt I needed to see Casey in all of his environments and relationships. As I had already seen him demonstrate in his visits with his parents and grandparents, it is normal for an infant or toddler to exhibit radically different attachment schemata and developmental capacities in the context of different caregiving relationships.

DISCUSSION

This context-dependent variability reflects the still-fluid and immature nature of the very young child's sense of self, which is, in Stern's (1985) words, emergent. There is a comparable quality in early speech and language: the babbling infant is able to make every known sound that occurs in any human language, while the 2-year-old has settled down to those used in his own native language. For the attuned therapist, this fluidity demands a matching flexibility anchored by a stable core sense of self so that the infant can experience being seen and held-in-mind in all his permutations by a containing "Other." This combination of flexibility and stability, in healthy attachment relationships, fosters the development of greater stability, containment, and coherence in the infant. In a case like this one, the therapist needs a comparable kind of holding — by her professional community — to avoid being overwhelmed by the incoherence to which she needs to attune.

QZ NARRATIVE RESUMED

Since Casey was living in a foster home, I needed to observe him there. The foster mother was highly experienced with medically fragile infants and had two other babies in the home in addition to Casey. She prided herself on her ability to manage all their medical and therapy appointments. She had a tight routine and her caregiving style, while pleasant and attentive, was businesslike and emotionally reserved. When I arrived, Casey looked at me briefly and then continued to play with a foster sibling. After a few minutes, he looked straight at me and appeared to dissociate. He stilled and sat frozen, with glazed eyes, for about a minute before he returned to play. The foster mother said she saw him do this occasionally, usually when he was around strangers or with a change in routine. His doctor did not consider it seizure activity. She went on to tell me that Casey had serious sleep problems. He woke at least every two hours, was restless, twitched, cried, and moaned in his sleep. His sleep was much worse the night after visits. While I was talking to his foster mother, I noted that Casey scanned the room frequently, as he played and even laughed a few times with the other infant. He was notably livelier than I had seen him before. He did not startle when the phone rang. There was no disruption of his play when his foster mother left the room to answer it. It appeared that Casey felt contained and supported by the foster home's consistency and attentiveness, but did far worse at night, alone in the dark.

Visits with his mother and father were twice a week, for two hours in the morning. At my recommendation, the three-way visits with both parents were eliminated, and each parent spent an hour with Casey to maximize the likelihood that Casey's needs would be front and center.

This was yet another example of the power accorded me by the social worker, as it was NOT the parents' preference. Often I waited in the parking lot to observe Casey's response to seeing his parents arrive together and to observe how they negotiated their reunion. Casey never showed any interest or pleasure at these reunions. His affect remained subdued but blandly pleasant. He consistently turned his head away from whichever parent, usually Ben, came to take him out of his car seat.

During his hour with his father, Casey settled into a pattern of falling asleep within minutes of Ben entering the room and staying asleep for the rest of the hour. When Ben left the room, he would wake up. During Daphne's hour, Casey would engage with her briefly, then become distressed and need to be soothed. His affect was usually subdued; even his distress cues were feeble. I tried to be as completely predictable as possible: to sit in the same spot for every visit and to follow the same routine. I would greet Casey when I entered but otherwise I did not initiate any interaction. Frequently, Casey would look at me and make brief eye contact and/or seek some physical contact with me, usually just brief touching, as he had in that early visit. This seemed to reassure him. He scanned the room almost constantly, alerting and startling to even faint noise from outside the room.

I planned to complete my initial assessment in time for the next court date, at which the evidence for and against keeping Casey in protective custody would be reviewed. Knowing that I would be going to court with this family, I used one of our consultation group meetings to process how to talk to Ben and Daphne about what I planned to say. My observations of Casey's disorganized attachment behavior, hypervigilance, sleep disturbance, and dissociative episodes clearly supported that he had been horribly traumatized psychologically as well as physically and that he was unable to experience either parent as a secure base. His extreme avoidance with his father left me with a firm conviction that he experienced Ben as a threat — a threat that a small child can only cope with by becoming unconscious, as fight/flight are not viable options. Daphne's difficulties acknowledging and responding to Casey's distress, combined with her maternal supportiveness of Ben, suggested that she had had, did have, and would have difficulties protecting Casey from his father.

I too found Ben frightening, but fortunately I had resources other than sleep. I needed support and reassurance to find the courage and confidence to be direct with him. MB and the consult group let me know they had full confidence in my conclusions, and also validated my anxiety. They wanted to know the time of the meeting, and all said they would be thinking of me. I told them I had resolved to tell Ben and Daphne exactly what I was reporting and recommending to the court. I reminded myself of the hints each parent had shown me of their own traumatized incoherence. If I was to have any hope of helping them repair the horrific trauma within their family, I must model the capacity to bear the harsh truth. MB reminded me that no one had spoken truth for Ben and Daphne when they were children, and that my plan to name Casey's trauma was not only in his best interest but also indirectly spoke to his parents' unresolved psychological wounds. Bolstered by this support, I arranged to meet with both parents, the social worker, and the court-appointed child advocate, without Casey. I felt filled with dread, both of the awful story I needed to tell and because I feared that Ben would become enraged and violent and that I would not be safe.

We met in the same room we used for visits. For safety, I kept the doors open and had the CPS supervisor watching through the one-way window. As the parents entered, Daphne was oddly cheerful and chatty and Ben looked haggard and frightening. He immediately told me he was having a hard time, that he was not sleeping, and that was having severe headaches. Feeling merciless, I suggested he see his doctor and stated that the purpose of our meeting today was for me to share my assessment of and recommendations for their family. I reminded them that this was information that would be provided to the court. When I felt I had their attention, I said that my assessment was that Casey met criteria for posttraumatic stress disorder. I explained the diagnosis, as I had several times before with each of them. With my heart in my mouth, I told them that watching how Casey acted with them led me to believe that Ben had hurt Casey and Daphne had failed to protect Casey. I explained that Casey knew and remembered how he was hurt. Ben began to argue that it was his grandmother Mary who hurt him. I cut him off and reminded them that there was evidence of a prior brain bleed as well as his fractured arm. I told them that Casey's behavior with Ben showed fear, while his behavior with his grandmother did not. Somehow, I kept my voice calm, steady, and firm. Daphne started crying and Ben was stony. Without argument or curiosity, they agreed to everything I said would need to happen for them to remain involved with their son. They resumed talking about how badly Ben was feeling. They left, holding hands, subdued but pleasant. I felt exhausted, nauseated, and hopeless. I did not see that there was any way I could help these parents become safe and sensitive caregivers for Casey.

DISCUSSION

For Casey, as for all infants, safety versus danger — physical survival versus injury and death — are the paramount contexts that trump all others. Recent evidence suggests that "in early trauma produced by attachment figures, the attachment system and mentalizing abilities operate in an inverse relation. That is, a hyperactivation of the attachment system induced by trauma dramatically reduces the capacity for mentalizing" (Cortina & Liotti, 2010).

MB and QZ and the other members of the consultation group repeatedly struggled to mentalize for ourselves how Casey's experience existed in his mind, before and after QZ understood it. These discussions also served to support and expand her capacity to mentalize Casey's all-but-unbearably painful and perilous perch at the edge between conscious awareness and dissociative, brain-injured unawareness. Fear and pain tend to reduce even an intact brain to mindless protoplasm; Casey had a severe closed head injury and a brain that continued to bleed in these first weeks of treatment. It was so difficult to stay aware that we all had to go back over and over again to remind ourselves of the precise nature of Casey's injuries and neurological condition; we simply could not bear to remember them.

We reflected together that, because an infant's mental universe is so colored by the behavior and affective communication of the caregiver, the match between the infant's subjective and objective reality is never perfect and may, in certain kinds of relationships, become perverse or paradoxical.

A child may be objectively in grave danger yet subjectively feel safe. This is often the case when parents deliberately shelter the child from awareness of harsh realities that lie outside the parents' control. In the Robert Benigni film *Life is Beautiful*, a father in a concentration camp both manages to hide his son from the Nazis and to hide the Nazis' murderous program from the little boy who believes, in his hiding place, that he is playing an exciting game with his father. Conversely, a child can live in fear of a sadistic caregiver who threatens and bullies and terrorizes him, even if no physical injury occurs. While evolutionary biology tells us that the attachment system evolved to improve the likelihood of survival for fragile infants while their oversized brains are organizing (Bowlby, 1969), the signaling components of the attachment system (e.g., reaching, crying, clinging, pursuing) have both subjective affective-kinesthetic dimensions and emergent mental representations. An infant learns to distinguish between feeling safe and feeling scared in the context of the caregiving environment. This is not exactly the same as being safe, or being in danger.

A traumatic injury or injuries inflicted by a caregiving parent places the child squarely in the state described by Main and Hesse (1990) as "fright without solution." The danger to the child and his protection from danger emanate from the same source, the relationship with the caregiver, and there is no way to "make sense," no way to organize a coherent response. Put in the language of current brain research, the hippocampus and the prefrontal cortex go offline and the child exhibits disorganized and incoherent responses to his caregivers and to his own need states.

Yet the power of Casey's biologically built-in seeking for a secure base is dramatically illustrated by his "finding" QZ and placing himself physically in her orbit in their first meeting. We struggled to define what QZ did to make herself so palpably available to him. She took control of the chaotic visit scene and must have conveyed in her voice, in the changes in the lighting and noise level that followed from her actions, maybe even in the way she smelled, the electrical charge from her skin, that she was both strong and safe. Actually, she subjectively felt helpless and frightened. But she knew, as Casey did not, that those were feelings and that she had the resources to manage them.

QZ NARRATIVE RESUMED

At the fact-finding hearing, the judge accepted my recommendations without exception. Casey was made a legal dependent of the state and ordered to remain in foster care. The parents were each to have two supervised one-hour visits a week at the protective services office. Once a week I joined visits to provide therapeutic services and continued my efforts to learn how capable Daphne and Ben were of becoming more responsive and protective of Casey. Each parent seemed stuck in a pattern of responding to him that exacerbated his distress and disorganization, rather than modulating it.

Daphne gasped loudly in alarm whenever Casey moved or did anything. She talked to him in a weak, pleading voice with an unvarying smile that seemed unrelated to anything. She rarely responded to his cues and was ineffective when she did respond. During one visit she played peek-a-boo with Casey by placing a blanket over her head while holding a stuffed bear. When she pulled the blanket off her face she made growling sounds and thrust the bear into Casey's face. As Casey's distress cues escalated she repeated this game. This reminded me of the behavior of disorganized parents described by Main and Hesse (1990) who growled at, stalked, and bared their teeth at their infants in "play." I told her to stop and pointed out his distress. She stopped but did nothing to comfort him. When I suggested he needed to be held, she picked him up and he pushed away from her. She put him down with a defeated, helpless expression.

Ben invariably began his segment of the visit by saying "Boo!" several times to Casey. Casey would startle, look at him, and then look away. He would become tense, start rocking, and then become agitated. Ben did not notice his distress. He stopped saying "Boo" when I told him to, and complied with my instructions to pick Casey up and comfort him. Casey fell asleep shortly after Ben picked him up and slept through the rest of the visit. As Casey slept, I attempted to help Ben think about his saying "Boo," but he had no insight or curiosity about why he did this. While he could see it distressed Casey, he had absolutely no idea why that was so. Despite our repeated discussions, despite my telling him over and over not to, he continued doing this week after week with the same result. Casey became distressed and then fell asleep. When Ben again said "Boo!" just minutes after I reminded him, before he entered the room, I did not try to hide my anger. I asked him why he kept doing this to Casey. He was surprised at the intensity of my response. He never again said "Boo" in the visits, but he continued to be loud and intrusive until Casey became sleepy. I felt persecuted by having to work with him, when it felt so hopeless and it was so painful to watch his effect on Casey.

These visits felt like a roller coaster ride that I dreaded. At times, Daphne seemed to be shifting, to be able to see and attune to Casey, but these moments were fleeting and then she would again become incapacitated and disconnected. Casey continued to fall asleep soon after his visit with Ben started. The social worker and Casey's court-appointed advocate often watched my visits through the one-way observation mirror. When I met with them, almost weekly, they expressed, simultaneously, that they were horrified by the parent-infant interactions, and yet they could not believe my interpretations of Casey's behaviors. They did not want to think that Casey remembered being injured in his parents' care. It was helpful to have my consultant remind me that, without support, most adults become disorganized themselves when exposed to a disorganized infant. She said that everyone has disorganized places within themselves that can be triggered by a baby like Casey. Drawing to the fullest on my own training, support, and fortitude, I tried to be predictable and emotionally available for Casey, knowing that my own disorganized places were being constantly triggered. I was careful not to intrude but showed him with my voice and my movements that I was seeing everything. When I did enter the interaction I carefully titrated my involvement to support him but not to divert him from Daphne. Often if I just touched his leg or back when he seemed about to collapse he would be able to continue. Over time he started seeking my support with his gaze. In a distressing moment he would fix his eyes on mine with great intensity. He needed to see me seeing him. I was careful to hold his gaze and to respond with an expression and sometimes a few words that informed him I was there with him.

Two months into our work together, Daphne frightened Casey by having a toy suddenly make noise and thrusting it into his face. He startled and began crying, harder and harder, while she did absolutely nothing to comfort him. I interpreted his cues for her and still she did nothing. Finally, Casey collapsed on the floor, trembling but quiet. Daphne picked him up but he flailed and arched away from her. I suggested she try rocking him and he finally settled as she sat in rocker with him. I told her I thought maybe Casey was frightened of her not responding when he was so distressed, that this might be even more frightening than the noisy toy. She started crying, acknowledging that this could be true. She said she knew she was sometimes too passive. There were other times she should have responded, she added. She went on to tell me that on the day that Casey was injured, she had had strong, foreboding feelings as she left him at home alone with Ben. She said Ben had not been doing well, and as she drove to her appointment that day, she kept thinking that she should turn around and go home, but she did not. I chose not to respond to her tearfulness, her desire for reassurance and comfort. I spoke to the strength and courage she showed in disclosing this and reminded her that there had been multiple assaults on Casey, and that he could not go home until she was consistently able to protect him. In retrospect, this exchange signaled a shift in Daphne, an emerging acceptance of what she needed to do to regain and protect her baby.

She moved quickly to start on anti-depressants and birth control — steps I had recommended since the beginning of our work together. She decided to take a weekend trip with her family, without Ben. He was unhappy about this but she said, for the first time, that she needed some time away from him. I began to tentatively hope that she could become an effective protector of her child, yet I tried to titrate my optimism by reminding myself how entrenched the patterns of abuse can be.

Court was looming. I met again with both parents the week before the dependency trial to share my assessment of their progress. This was not as hard as the first time, as I was feeling more familiar with this stern, confrontational persona I used to speak to them about Casey's safety. I told them that while they had made some positive changes, Casey remained highly stressed in their presence. He both wanted to be near them and was afraid of them. I repeated that his behavior told me that he remembered that he was injured in their care. I added that I believed that each of them had significant psychological and domestic violence issues that needed treatment before Casey could be safe with them. I would be recommending to the court that he remain in his foster home and continue to have only supervised visits. Then, I reminded them that dependency law gave them a limited time before they faced termination of their parental rights. I affirmed that I saw how much they loved Casey and urged them to work hard to learn how to be safe caregivers for him. I added that I would continue to work with them in the visits. They responded with disbelief, anger, and tears, while blaming each other. This was another sign that their bond with one another was under tension. Interestingly, they did not attack me, as I had feared. The next week they agreed to the dependency and the trial was cancelled.

DISCUSSION

In consultation, we talked about the many affective and behavioral stances that QZ needed to keep available in working this case. The confrontation and directiveness she used with Ben and Daphne demanded courage and toughness; the emotional availability she offered to Casey demanded psychological openness and vulnerability. In court, she needed to find an objective, rational, and dispassionate voice. In the protected world of private practice, the multiple roles she was playing, as therapist, evaluator, and legal advocate would be challenged, perhaps viewed as dual relationships. In the resource-poor world of child welfare, with a child whose life was literally on the line, any attempts to circumscribe her efforts felt immoral. That did not make balancing the multiple roles any easier. In this context, having a support group that could help her think and help her stay organized and maintain psychological integrity was critical. No one can think clearly while on such a psychological rollercoaster.

QZ NARRATIVE RESUMED

In the following two months, visits continued to be wildly inconsistent and distressing. At that point, a new challenge arose. The criminal investigation cleared both Daphne and her mother, but Ben was charged with first-degree felony assault of a child. He was enraged and unable to contain this during his visits. Ben spent his visits rocking rapidly in the rocking chair while Casey slept in his arms. He insisted to me that grandmother Mary was the one who hurt Casey. Although I reminded him that I was working for the state and that what he told me was not confidential, he poured out his anger and distress as Casey slept in his arms. He spoke insistently about his own traumatic childhood, describing severe and random beatings and serious head injuries when no one took him to the hospital. When I asked how this had affected him, he said that he gets really bad migraines. As an afterthought, he added that when he gets really angry he sometimes blacks out and hurts people. I felt both sick and relieved to be hearing this almost-confession. It made me very sad for Ben, and more scared than ever for Casey and Daphne.

Soon after Ben was charged, Daphne, with her usual all-purpose smile, told me that Ben had ended their relationship. She was now living with her mother. During this first visit after the break-up, she was more animated and Casey responded to her with brightened affect and more babbling. She was better able to redirect him and help him remain focused in his play. I suggested she take the cushions off the sofa and make a mountain for him to climb. She did this, and they both laughed as he climbed the mountain and rolled down. He became overexcited and I coached her through calming him and setting limits on the climbing. I saw how timid she was about setting limits, even around Casey's safety, and suggested she think of herself as a mother bear. Mother bear will do anything to protect her cub, whether by limit setting, nurturing, or by fiercely fighting off predators. Daphne seemed to be intrigued with this image of herself as a bear protecting her cub. Mother bear became our shorthand in coaching her through difficult moments in the visits. When I described this metaphor to the consultation group, MB said she thought I was describing myself!

Casey was now 16 months old. He continued to have flat affect and rarely cried. He was mostly silent, making occasional guttural noises with communicative intent. He had significant oral motor dysfunction, including swallowing challenges. His play was restless and unfocused, although there were islands of connection and positive affect during his visits w Daphne. He continued to fall into a sleep unrelated to fatigue in every visit with his father. I consistently sat in the same spot. I acknowledged Casey and kept him in my attention but rarely initiated interaction. I wanted to nurture his relationship with his mother rather than build a relationship between him and me. We had a ritual greeting where he would come up to me, lean on my knee, look at me, and vocalize. I would say my name and pat my chest. Then he found my badge and again I would say my name and pat the photo as well as my chest. Then we would do this with his name and pat his chest. He smiled as we repeated this several times at the start of each visit. I began to feel he was ready to make use of some symbolic play to tell me more about his world. I brought a little green caterpillar puppet that I called Wormy Guy who could be raised up and down on a stick, hiding in his apple or popping up to say hello. Casey was immediately fascinated by Wormy Guy. I always held Wormy Guy and narrated his comings and goings to Casey. Over several visits we developed some play routines, such as having Wormy Guy say good bye and go to sleep and then wake up and be hungry. Casey started laughing out loud while playing with Wormy Guy and started giving him kisses. He would offer him toys and food. Over time I brought other toys but Wormy Guy remained the favorite.

DISCUSSION

Both these interactive games with QZ serve to help Casey build a stable sense of self and other and to master the many comings and goings of his brief life. Yet with exquisite tact, QZ remained in a subsidiary role, serving not as a replacement for his mother but rather as a prosthesis for the parts of his mother that were deficient or wounded. The power of the pull the therapist feels to offer oneself as a replacement attachment figure to an endangered and engaging infant cannot be overestimated; in infant mental health, it is a countertransference pitfall at least as dangerous as are sexual countertransferences in psychotherapy with adults (Birch, 2008). The risk is heightened by the ways in which the therapist may be called upon, as QZ was, to play an active advocacy role. Consultation may be essential to support a consistent therapeutic stance, keeping one's goals and hopes firmly rooted in the child's real situation, not in a fantasied rescue with oneself as the replacement parent.

QZ NARRATIVE RESUMED

Daphne was becoming more responsive to and less tentative with Casey. Her pacing now matched his and their play became livelier. Casey sought much more physical contact with her, and accepted hugs and cuddles that she offered. He also displayed some mild temper for the first time, and Daphne responded appropriately, validating his feelings but setting limits when needed for his safety. When he gave her a kiss — the first time ever — she and I were both a little tearful. When I commented on his growing positive responses to her, Daphne responded that she felt less tense without Ben in her life. I responded that Casey was starting to feel safe with her, safe enough to get mad and know she would keep them both safe. Daphne smiled when I said this, a real smile. I too was beginning to have faith in Daphne, faith that felt as fragile as a bubble.

When I met with Daphne alone, to check in on the rest of her life, she told me she had continued on anti-depressant medication, which seemed to be helping, and had enrolled in a six-month technical program that would give her the skills to financially support herself and Casey. She was planning to move into an apartment with her sister, who was also in school. When I brought up the issue of dating, Daphne said she was not ready to have another man in her life. She just wanted to focus on being a mother and going to school.

I was even more impressed a week later when Daphne was able to graciously but tearfully accept that it might be less stressful for Casey if his foster mother, with whom he had now been living for six months, was the one to be with him in the hospital during a scheduled surgery.

I told her that I was close to recommending that she have unsupervised visits and that she be allowed to go to Casey's routine medical appointments. However, I still needed evidence that she was working to learn about her failure to protect Casey from Ben, and her enmeshment with Ben. She told me she was starting in a Domestic Violence group next month and would be starting individual counseling soon. She said she knew she had her difficulties with relationships and needed to make changes.

Casey began to have his visits with Daphne supervised by the maternal grandparents, Mary and Bill, in their home. If these went well, he would be moved from foster care to this relative placement. I suggested that Daphne and Mary be required to start family therapy together to work through the tensions in their relationship so they could work together on Casey's behalf. Mary held some resentment and distrust from Daphne's involvement with Ben and early support of his accusations that she, Mary, had hurt Casey. On Daphne's side, she was just beginning to sort out the impact that Mary's alcoholism during her childhood had had on her and how it still colored their relationship despite a decade of recovery. On my first visit to the grandparents' home, I was stunned to see the difference in Casey. He was joyful, focused, and calm. He was not hypervigilant and not particularly distressed by people coming and going. However, he was clumsier than usual, which might have indicated that he was still feeling some stress. When Daphne needed to use the bathroom, she told him where she was going. He followed her and waited outside the door, talking to her. He seemed to be relaxed, and confident. When it was time for Casey to return to his foster home, Daphne and Mary each held him, gave him kisses and hugs, and told him they would see him soon. Daphne carried him out to the car and Casey waved goodbye.

I was worried that Ben could be threatening, violent, and might try to forcibly take Casey when he learned of the plan to place Casey with the grandparents. Mary and Bill lived in a remote rural area, with no cell phone service and no close neighbors, and it would be a long wait for police response if needed. Daphne said she did not think Ben would actually do anything, which I thought showed her continued denial. Her sister strongly disagreed and alluded to some scary incidents in the past. Mary and Bill agreed that Ben was really a scary guy and owned guns. We had a family meeting to create a safety plan. I had them write out the safety plan and post it on the refrigerator. Daphne agreed that if Ben came to the home she would call 911 and then escape into the woods. Mary created a backpack with extra clothes, food, and a cell phone, and they kept this by the back door.

DISCUSSION

As QZ's consultant, MB repeatedly asked her to detail her own safety plan. Her active advocacy role and her relationship with Ben put her potentially in the crosshairs of his rage. With this in mind, she made it a practice to notify law enforcement when she went on a home visit to the grandparents' home and when she left, and to keep her colleagues in the public health department aware of her schedule. We repeatedly reviewed Ben's criminal history and the nature of the assaults he had committed.

QZ NARRATIVE RESUMED

Over the next month Casey transitioned to longer visits at the grandparents. Daphne was attending his speech therapy appointments and told me with pride that she insisted to the therapist that Casey needed her to be in the room with him during his therapy. It was hard because she knew the therapist preferred her to stay in the waiting room, and her habit was to defer to authority, but she spoke up because she felt Casey needed her to be there.

On the day of Casey's first overnight visit, Daphne, her sister, grandmother Mary, and I sat watching Casey play and talking about sleep management. As we talked, Casey began making guttural but happy sounds while jumping vigorously up and down as Mary held him under his arms. She was sitting in a chair and he was standing on the floor in front of her. He would not bear weight on his legs, although by now he was an accomplished walker. He jumped with great gusto, making Mary support his weight as he came back to earth. He did this again and again, stopping and looking, long and deep, at each of us in turn, before jumping and grunting again. We all laughed at him but were puzzled. I think we all felt he was trying to tell us something. Suddenly, Mary exclaimed that she knew exactly what he was doing. He was pretending to be in his Johnny Jump Up bouncer, which had been his favorite game to play with Mary when she would babysit him in the months before his injury. She said she would always sit in the same chair she was in now, and his bouncer was in the doorway beside her chair. Fortunately I had my new video camera in my pocket and started filming. Casey only stopped this game after we all agreed that HE WAS TELLING US HE REMEMBERED. As he moved on to play with toys, I interpreted this to the family as clear indicator that he had memory of his infancy, both good and bad events, before the abuse, and most likely of the abuse and that he needed them to see this truth. This was a profound moment for Daphne and Mary. Although I had said many times that his behavior showed he had the capacity to remember, they (like the social worker and the child advocate) had been reluctant to believe me until now. I was also moved and relieved by Casey's reenactment. It seems so radical to believe a baby has a memory, especially when he has a traumatic brain injury. At times I had thought maybe I was wrong, was imagining things. I had to admire Casey's persistence and brilliance in finding a way to convince us all. Daphne, Mary, and I discussed the imminent anniversary of Casey's abuse. They now believed that Casey remembered and that his mind held a story of what happened to him. I explained that even infants seem to know anniversaries and he would need their support. Daphne immediately accepted this, and suggested they take him to the fire station to meet the paramedics and look at the aid car. I was proud of her ability to come up with a plan that would make sense to a toddler and let him know that she also remembered.

DISCUSSION

In this phase of the treatment, QZ added the roles of play therapist, family therapist, and safety planner to the earlier roles of advocate, visit supervisor, forensic evaluator, attachment facilitator, and developmental counselor. In consultation, we reflected on the striking tension between her firm, active, directive stance and her ongoing inner doubts and distrust of her own observations. Surrounded by adults who were unable to believe that Casey's mind was capable of remembering and representing his experiences, she gained confidence when Casey himself was able to mirror and validate her observations in a way even his mother and grandmother could not gainsay. QZ also needed support to titrate her fears and hopes about progress. As we see below, Daphne's capacity for denial was by no means completely vanquished even at this point. The delay in communicating with QZ about the new injury and her dependence on QZ to mentally link it to Casey's behavior changes showed how fragile her gains were.

QZ NARRATIVE RESUMED

Two weeks later I was surprised when Daphne told me Casey had been very upset, whining, clinging, kicking, hitting, and biting for a few days. After several minutes of speculating about the behavior that Casey was demonstrating as we talked, Daphne suggested, casually, as an afterthought, that it might be because Ben had dropped him on his head during a visit. I nearly fell out of my chair onto my own head! I called MB after this session, and she said exactly the same thing. Daphne said that Casey was taken to the hospital emergency room and seemed to be okay. I was stunned by this news and by the offhanded manner with which Daphne shared it. Even more disturbing, I suddenly realized that I myself had totally forgotten about the anniversary, even though we had talked at our last meeting about preparing for it. I felt so confused that I had to get out my papers and review the dates to be certain. As we reviewed the time frames it became clear that Ben had dropped Casey on his head within 12 hours of the one-year anniversary of his original head injury. This occurred during a supervised visit, and the observing visit supervisor had not intervened in any way. It was Mary, not anyone from protective services, who had taken Casey to the emergency room when she picked him up after the visit. No one, it seemed, could bear to think about or know what Casey was experiencing.

As I drove away I felt flooded with anxiety and dread, thinking about Casey going back into the visit room, alone with Ben. I was horrified by our collective incapacity to think clearly and protect him. I drove until I got to an area with cell reception and called MB. I told her about the incident. MB was appropriately distressed also. She pointed out that the potential danger was not only from Ben's violence but also from the disorganizing impact this threat had on Casey's other caregivers, including me, making it harder for us to protect him effectively. She felt no doubt that this accidental yet perfectly synchronistic dropping Casey on his head was Ben's frightening way of remembering what he still could not acknowledge consciously. I told her that I wanted to initiate a petition to stop Ben's visits. She told me to go ahead. I immediately called the social worker, who called the attorney general, and court was scheduled for two days later. The morning before court, I presented the situation to our consult group. I remember feeling intensely anxious and sad as I described the events. It helped a little that the group members all supported me and confirmed my sense of urgency. Unfortunately, the threat that seemed so clear to us was not successfully communicated to the judge. Court was a disaster. Ben's attorney grilled me for an hour, challenging the credibility of my interpretation of the accident, and the attorney general did nothing to support the petition. The judge ruled that Ben's visits would continue. As a final blow, the judge reprimanded me because I had ended Ben's sessions when he insisted that they be videotaped, and I was court-ordered to resume work with Ben and be videotaped. I left feeling that I had totally failed to protect Casey.

DISCUSSION

Containment is the creation of what Sandler called "the background of safety" (1960), Winnicott (1960) called "the holding environment," and Fonagy et al. described as "the creation of an interpersonal situation where the potential for reflective function could be specifically and safely exercised" (2002, p. 403). In infant mental health, containment is not only a psychological 'holding the infant in mind' (Slade, 2002). Pragmatically, it entails creating and maintaining the conditions where it becomes possible to address and explore higher-order intersubjective themes, because primal themes, like survival, are not in question. Chronic hyperarousal of the attachment system (called "fright without solution" by Main & Hesse, 1990) leads to the collapse of advanced intersubjective capacities. However, when the attachment behavioral system is not chronically activated by fear and abandonment, it can become integrated with the infant's emergent intersubjective capabilities. "Even when we are alone, every single perception that emerges in higher order consciousness becomes conscious from the perspective of being potentially communicable to another human being" (Cortina & Liotti, 2010, p. 430). Early unresolved trauma often leads to disorganized attachment (Solomon & George, 1999). The disorganized child is chronically hypervigilant and preoccupied with safety. He or she uses one of two kinds of defensive detours to manage the chronic activation of unmet attachment needs and terror. Both strategies reflect an effort to control the unpredictable and dangerous love object. The first is to become compulsively and precociously caregiving to the frightened and/or frightening caregiver. The second is to become aggressive and punitive in an attempt to bully and dominate the frightened and/or frightening caregiver. It may be useful to see each of Casey's parents as showing one of the two complementary forms of the 'controlling' strategy to manage disorganized attachment. This is a common feature of violent domestic partnerships (Lyons-Ruth, 1999; Crittenden, 2008).

Casey's mother initially inhibits activation of her attachment system by engaging in compulsive caregiving for her primary love object, father Ben. Father inhibits activation of his disorganized attachment system by being domineering and bullying with mother. When Casey is born, his primitive, undefended attachment behaviors and signals place unbearable demands on the fragile Rube Goldberg-like system of emotional checks and balances in his parents' relationship. "When the conditions for the activation of the attachment system are sufficiently prolonged or intense, the relative inhibition by the defensive activation of the caregiving or the dominance-ranking systems may be overcome. The disorganized representation of the attachment relationship may then be activated with its cohort of sometimes dramatic, frightening, dissociative experiences" (Cortina & Liotii, 2010, p. 433). When QZ enters this disorganized, incoherent system, her own attachment system is continuously activated and she must vigorously recruit all of her internal and external strategies for maintaining enough equilibrium to think, or at least enough equilibrium to know she cannot think.

QZ NARRATIVE RESUMED

Driving to the first visit after court, I was very tired and felt like a total failure. I felt a profound and hopeless dread about Casey continuing visits with Ben. My ideas about how to coach the family to support Casey before and after visits — visits that I felt and I believed Casey experienced as life-threatening — seemed totally inadequate. Daphne and Mary were very subdued, and our shared feeling of despair was palpable. Oddly, Casey seemed talkative and cheerful. We played with Wormy Guy for a few minutes, as we always did. When he moved on to play with his other toys Daphne and I started discussing what had happened at court. As if he knew exactly what we were talking about, Casey's demeanor immediately changed. He became clingy, screaming, flailing when held but refusing to be put down. Mary took him into another room so Daphne and I could talk. She told me how hard it was to send him to visits when she now knew that he remembered what happened to him. I acknowledged how hard it was, and coached her in the small part of a painful and scary situation that she could control: about how she could understand and tolerate his distress and acting out, talking to him about visits, and keeping his routine as dependable as possible. This paralleled the coaching I had received from my consultant, who reminded me of the overwhelming odds this case presented and helped me to keep refocusing on the small things I could do, rather than how pitiably futile they felt.

Later I met with the social worker and court child advocate. We all felt terribly defeated by the court decision. We were terrified that the criminal trial, in barely two months, would end with Ben being acquitted of all charges. As the best of a bad set of options, we decided to seek an immediate in-home dependency with Daphne. We were particularly concerned that acquittal would open the door for Ben's lawyers to ask for unsupervised visits or shared custody. I worried that Daphne was still too vulnerable to Ben. She had only been separated from him for a few months, and was just starting to work on her domestic violence issues. The plan also meant another transition for Casey. The social worker again asked me to tell Daphne about this plan. I think she felt sorry for me after the court disaster. Despite all my doubts, it did feel good to share some good news with Daphne after all the distressing things I had had to tell her.

She was thrilled. I told her my concerns about this plan. I did not doubt her ability to parent Casey, but I worried about her ability to stay away from Ben, and to stand up to him if she needed to. Daphne told me not to worry about that, that she was very much over him. She agreed that Ben would be angry, but despite all that had happened, she was certain he would not do anything scary when he learned Casey was living with her. I felt dismayed and could not believe she was still in denial about Ben's potential for violence. This rushed transition was far from ideal and there was a real risk of Daphne's collapse into helplessness. For some time now, I had taken a more traditional therapeutic stance with Daphne, following her lead, but now I decided to be more directive with her again, to model the Mother Bear stance. I told her that she needed to actively practice asserting herself, so she would be able to cope with Ben's intimidation. I told her that I expected her to start arguing with me, to start disagreeing with my suggestions, with my interpretations, as a way to build her stamina for conflict and support her growth as a protective Mother Bear. Daphne seemed a little confused by this but agreed she would try. I also said there could be no more delays in starting her own individual therapy. Daphne told me she had joined an online support group around Shaken Baby Syndrome and had started to talk to her friends about what had really happened to Casey. I supported this but insisted she needed individual therapy to explore her relationship with Ben, her inability to listen to her own feelings and protect Casey. This time she followed through immediately and began treatment.

As Casey began transitioning to Daphne's home with a series of lengthening visits monitored by me or Mary, I focused on practical, concrete issues: how to childproof her apartment, how to join the community mother-infant play group, how to apply for food assistance, and how to manage her busy schedule of classes and appointments. Together we completed Casey's developmental screening. He was still significantly delayed in speech and social emotional development but showed only borderline delays in gross and fine motor skills. I tried to normalize the transition, to offer assistance that any new mother might need and want. I certainly also felt relief in getting a break from being immersed in trauma and dread.

Daphne told me that she observed that, after visits with Ben, Casey would put everything into his mouth, was restless with a very short attention span, and woke several times at night crying. We explored ways she could talk to Casey about his visits with Ben to allow him to anticipate what would be happening and to validate his feelings of anxiety and distress, while reassuring him that he would come home to her. Daphne said she was angry that Ben had cancelled so many visits. It was disruptive to Casey's routine and undermined her efforts to prepare him for visits. I commented to her on her choice of the word angry — rare for her — and the congruence between her affect and that word. She had little insight into this shift, but she was pleased I noticed.

On our next visit Casey had little interest in playing with me as he usually did at the beginning of visits. He was interested in me, greeted me as he usually did but spent the visit playing contentedly with his own toys. He seemed more lively than usual. Daphne informed me he had hit her a few times, as well as thrown some toys. She was upset by this behavior and told me she did not know how to respond to him. I tried to help her think about why Casey might be feeling angry now, but she seemed too overwhelmed to think about it. I suggested that Casey might be feeling safe enough with her, that he trusted her to both protect him and to not fall apart when he shared his more difficult feelings with her. This seemed to click and Daphne compared this to how she and her mother were finally able to talk about their conflicts in their therapy sessions. We closed the visit by discussing how much progress she had made in our work together.

A few visits later, Daphne told me Casey was sleeping better, less stressed after visits with his father, and was less aggressive. He had started to have temper tantrums and to resist her efforts to get him to do things like lie still for diaper changes. When I asked what she thought of these changes, Daphne responded that she had really worked to change how she talked to him about visits. After visits she now asked him, "How was his visit," instead of asking if he had a good visit. I agreed this gave him more room to tell her how he felt. She was also being more consistent about his routine. She was delighted with my praise for these changes and pleased that I remarked that he was starting to act like a typical almost 2-year-old. I reminded her, again, that he had not forgotten his abuse and that, despite the wonderful gains we were both seeing, he would continue to need support as the trauma surfaced in different ways throughout his lifetime. I suggested that it was time to shift our focus. Casey was doing well and telling me he felt safe with his mother and that he did not need our therapeutic play. I suggested she and I start meeting alone to help prepare her emotionally for her testimony at the criminal trial in 2 months. I also reminded Daphne that our visits would stop when the dependency was closed. I briefly felt disappointed when she didn't seem sad at the thought of our work together ending.

In the one-on-one meetings that followed, Daphne and I were able to continue talking about Casey's anger, how he sometimes needed to be angry at her for not protecting him. Daphne could listen to me say this but she couldn't discuss this. She did express her fear that Ben might eventually be granted partial custody of Casey. We revisited my failure in court to protect Casey.

In an effort to help her feel strong and able to endure what was sure to be hours of brutal questioning and cross-examination, I reminded Daphne of her successes of the last year. She was about to graduate from her training program with excellent grades and a promised job, she has Casey in her home, and she had left an abusive relationship. I also asked Daphne to consider what she has lost in the last year. She became tearful as we discussed how she had missed Casey's first birthday and his first steps and was not there to care for him when he had surgery. She expanded on this, adding she had missed out on her family's support because Ben had wanted them to move away while she was pregnant. I told Daphne that if she had stayed in this community for her pregnancy and Casey's birth that I could have been her home visiting nurse, to support her through these transitions, just like I did with other first time mothers in the community. I told her that I was sad we did not get that chance to work together. We talked about how her life might have been different if she had had support and information instead of being isolated. Tearfully, Daphne stated she thought she would have known that Ben was dangerous and would have left him before Casey was hurt. We sat together in a poignant silence, grieving for that missed opportunity.

The week before Ben's trial Daphne told me that the prosecuting attorney and the victims advocate asked her to consider agreeing to a plea bargain for Ben. The plan was that, if he pleaded guilty to third degree felony assault of a child with a domestic violence and weapons tag, he would not spend any time in jail. Hearing this, I was outraged and expressed my disgust that this would let Ben walk away without any punishment and that I thought he deserved jail time. Daphne was calm and confident as she told me that she was in favor of the plea bargain, although her family and I all opposed it and wanted to see Ben punished. She understood why we felt this, but, she added, her primary goal was to make sure Casey was safe. I am sure that I looked shocked at this statement. Daphne went on to tell me the reasons why this was a good decision. She explained that the prosecutor informed her that, with this record of felony assault, no court would ever allow Ben to be alone with Casey. He would never be granted custody or even unsupervised visits. Daphne thought Ben would eventually go away if he knew he could never get Casey back and, once the dependency was closed, he would have to arrange and pay for supervised visits. Daphne said she was angry that the trade-off was that he would not serve time, but that this was the best way for her to keep Casey safe. If it went to trial, she had no guarantee that he would not be acquitted. I felt incredibly proud of her at that moment. I told her that I thought she was seeing this more clearly than the rest of us. I was proud of her being such a great mother bear, for figuring this out, and for arguing with me. She beamed, as she responded that she was also proud of herself for finally finding her strength. MB remarked when I reported this exchange that perhaps my 'failure' had helped make room for Daphne's strength.

The plea bargain was entered and we continued with the termination phase of our work, closing as planned. I receive periodic updates from Daphne, who tells me that Casey continues to do very well. He has graduated from all of his early intervention services. If you saw him playing with other kids, you would not guess the trauma he has endured.

Three years later, with Casey still safe and developing normally, his case feels seared into my brain.

CONCLUSION

When a therapist such as QZ is engaged on behalf of an infant whose life is in real danger, and who lacks any fully committed and competent caregiver, she must somehow distinguish her healthy, protective impulses, triggered by her mature caregiving behavioral system, from impulses that are rooted in compulsive caregiving or dominant/punitive efforts to prevent the activation of the disorganized elements in her own representation of the attachment relationship. Furthermore, in the countertransference, she experiences the complementary feelings to the parents' internal representations of relationship — such as fear, utter confusion, rage, intense anxiety, and so forth. No one, including QZ and her consultation group, as evidenced by the instances of forgetting what is in plain sight, wants to know what QZ is seeing. In addition, she is pressured in different ways by the judge, the social worker, the family, and herself ("I wondered if I was imagining all this"). How does a therapist work on all these levels with integrity and without fragmentation?

When they meet, Casey's existence, both as a living child, and as an emergent self, is in extreme peril. He is held together only by the external scaffolding provided by his medical providers (the protective helmet, medication, prescribed low-stimulation sensory diet) and the child welfare system (a safe foster home, supervised visits) and the legal system (protective custody, criminal investigation and adjudication). Having experienced extreme states of pain and fear, Casey embodies Donald Winnicott's oft-quoted dictum that "there is no such thing as a baby" (1960). In other words, when QZ meets him, Casey does not exist because there is no one, no environment, no caregiver, that is able to see, mirror, and respond contingently to him. If a tree falls in the forest, does it make a sound? If your mother leaves you over and over with someone who hurts you and scares you, if you climb up into her lap over and over and she puts you back on the floor with your back to her, and says, "I don't know how to hold my baby" — do you exist?

All infants, like Casey, seek and recognize when they are being held in another's mind the way a plant seeks light, and like plants without light, without such containment, infants' minds die. One way to define QZ's challenge — our challenge — in working with traumatized infants is to define our work as finding ways to provide both "real" and "felt" safety. This goal is pursued not only by understanding and mirroring but also by modes of containment that are at times concrete, directive, and even not nice. These included:

- Telling it like it is, telling people things they do not want to hear
- Physical instructions – how to hold Casey to stop his tremor
- Setting limits, dictating visit formats, taking charge
- Making rules about noise, light, activity levels
- Coaching Daphne how to fight
- Establishing routines and rituals
- Active involvement and advocacy in court, placement decisions
- Narrating Casey's experience to others
- Fostering representational play (Wormy Guy)
- Communicating physical and emotional availability to Casey without being intrusive or disrespectful of parents

We continually see evidence in this work with traumatized patients of our own need for containing relationships and institutions as we try to think about and communicate about our work. For example, QZ initially felt completely blocked as she tried to write up this story. After a ten-minute phone conversation in which MB articulated and confirmed the impossibility of "saying everything there is to say" and suggested that this paper was only one of many possible ways to tell the story, her block completely lifted. Though less dramatic, this is the same containing advice that MB gave earlier about staying focused on small things she could actually accomplish to avoid being flooded by anxiety about the unknown. In the course of this work, QZ used consultation to help her know what she was thinking when she couldn't hear her own voice, to help her formulate how to proceed in the face of intense feelings of hopelessness and powerlessness by focusing on assessment and harm reduction, and to help her find a clinical rationale for doing things that felt mean or bossy. She felt, at times, intensely sick, disgusted, persecuted, pressured, powerless, omnipotently responsible, helpless, harsh, mean, scared, incompetent, persecuted, unable to think, forgetful, and, most of all, overwhelmed. These are normal responses to being emotionally available to traumatized infants and disorganized family systems, and they make containing relationships and institutions a necessity, not a luxury in infant mental health.

ACKNOWLEDGMENTS

We would like to express our gratitude to Dott Kelly, MA, and William Maier, MSW, the other members of the consultation group referred to above, for their unflagging and brilliant support for this work.

REFERENCES

Birch, M. (2008). The reason for such a book. In M. Birch (Ed.), *Finding hope in despair: Clinical studies in infant mental health* (pp.1–28). Washington, DC: Zero to Three Press.

Bowlby, J. (1969). *Attachment*. NY: Basic Books.

Cortina, M., & Liotti, G. (2010). Attachment is about safety and protection, intersubjectivity is about sharing and social understanding. *Psychoanalytic Psychology*, *27*, 413–441.

Crittenden, P. M. (2008). *Raising parents: attachment, parenting and child safety*. Devon, UK: Willan.

DC: 0-3R/Diagnostic Classification of Mental Health and Developmental Disorders of Infancy and Early Childhood: Revised Edition. (2005). Washington, DC: Zero to Three Press

Fonagy, P., Gergely, G., Jurist, E. L., & Target, M. (2002). *Affect regulation, mentalization and the development of the self*. New York, NY: Other Press.

Greenspan, S., & Weider, S. (2000). Principles of clinical practice for assessment & intervention. In *Clinical practice guidelines: Redefining the standards of care for infants, children & families with special needs* (pp. 55–82). Bethesda, MD: The Interdisciplinary Council on Developmental and Learning Disorders.

Lyons-Ruth, K., Bronfman, E., & Atwood, G. (1999). A relational diathesis model of hostile-helpless states of mind: Expressions in mother-infant interaction. In J. Solomon & C. George (Eds.), *Attachment disorganization* (pp. 33–70). New York, NY: Guilford Press.

Main, M., & Hesse, E. (1990). Parents' unresolved traumatic experiences are related to infant disorganized attachment status: Is frightened and/or frightening parental behavior the linking mechanism? In M.T. Greenberg, D. Cicchetti, & E.M. Cummings (Eds.), *Attachment in the preschool years: Theory, research & intervention* (pp. 161–182). Chicago, IL: University of Chicago Press.

Olds, D. L., Eckenrode, J., Henderson, C. R., Kitzman, H.,Powers, J., Cole, R., ... Lucky, D. (1997). Long-term effects of home visitation on maternal life course and child abuse and neglect. *The Journal of the American Medical Association*, *278*, 637–643.

Pawl, J. (1995). Therapeutic relationship as human connectedness: Being held in another's mind. *Zero to Three*, *15*, 3–5.

Sandler, J. (1960). The background of safety. *International Journal of Psychoanalysis*, *41*, 352–356.

Schafer, R. (1976). *A new language for psychoanalysis*. New Haven, CT: Yale University Press,

Slade, A. (2002). *Keeping baby in mind*. Zero to Three.

Solomon, J. & George, C. (Eds.). (1999). *Attachment disorganization*. NY: Guilford Press.

Stern, D. (1985). *The interpersonal world of the infant*. NY: Basic Books.

Winnicott D. W. W. (1960). The theory of the infant-parent relationship. *International Journal of Psychoanalysis*, *41*, 585–595.

Winnicott, D. W. W. (1963). Fear of breakdown. In C. Winnicott, R. Shepherd, & M. Davis (Eds.) (1989) *Psychoanalytic explorations* (pp. 87–95). Cambridge, MA: Harvard University Press.

APPENDIX A: BREATHING EXERCISE FOR ANXIETY

Sit up straight so that you are not leaning against your seat back. Rest your hands in your lap in whatever way is comfortable for you. Gently close your eyes, or look down at your lap with a soft focus. Repeat 10 times:

- Inhale 2 *3*4
- Hold 2*3*4
- Exhale 2*3*4*5*6*7*8
- Hold 2*3*4 3min
- Repeat ten times, using your fingers to count repetitions.
- Take a moment to notice your internal state after this exercise. As we continue our story, please remember to be mindful of your own internal process.

The "Dead Mother Syndrome" and the Child in Care: A Framework for Reflecting on Why Some Children Experience Multiple Placement Breakdowns

Carolyn Hart

This paper is concerned with a subset of children in foster care who present as unable to use resources available to them. They make individuals involved with them feel inadequate and useless. Perhaps as a result of this, even from toddler-hood, these children experience serial disruption of foster placements. It is suggested that using Green's (1986) concept of the "dead mother syndrome" (whereby a child experiences a mother as physically present but emotionally dead) provides a useful framework to support both individual psychodynamic psychotherapy with the child and also a range of work with the team around the child.

INTRODUCTION

From time to time, I imagine that we all have clients that we find perplexing, who make us feel inadequate and useless; clients who make us question our ability to do the work. Paul, a 12-year-old boy in foster care who also had learning difficulties, was one such client for me. Truthfully, my own feelings of inadequacy made me feel so uncomfortable that I would have preferred not to work with him. When I was with him, I felt so inadequate that it was easy to rationalize that my skills would be better used with a different client. The temptation to abandon him, and likewise my feelings of incompetence, were huge.

Paul, in contrast, at the start of each session seemed eager to see me. As he caught sight of me coming to the waiting room, he would bound down the corridor to greet me with a clumsy all-embracing bear hug. Yet, by the time we had entered the therapy room, I would feel that my only use was to pass him items he may require.

Typically, Paul would stand just inside the door and metaphorically take a proprietary stroll around his room. His gaze would fall on one item after another. He might start at the table with the paint and move around the room naming each item. It felt as if each session started with an inventory of things at his disposal. I was such an item. There would always be a singsong, emotionally flat commentary such as:

> "There's the paint: red, yellow, green-I like green. I might use that later. Yellow and blue make green. There's yellow play-dough in my box- oh look more paper today and there's the doll's house and the sand, pass me the water . . . I'm going to do some mixing today. I wonder where the cars are. Oh in the box. I'm going to play in the sand . . ."

This commentary would continue for the duration of every session, and I felt as if there was no space for me, it was as if I did not exist. I began to feel that Paul's commentary was designed to keep me out, keep me at a distance, and prevent us from engaging in any kind of meaningful, effective exchange. On the few occasions that I managed to utter a thought along these lines, he would stop momentarily, look at me, state that he "needed me," and instantaneously go back to what he was doing and restart the commentary.

I now recognize this scenario as being typical of a subset of children in foster care who experience serial placement breakdown and whose behavior can be explained through an understanding of the "dead mother syndrome" (Green, 1986).

Placement breakdowns are common. Newton et al. (2000) found that disruptions in foster care placements were associated with increases in both externalizing and internalizing child behavior problems. The U.S. Department of Health and Human Services (2005) reported on data collected in 2002, which indicated that 73% of the children in the United States who were in care longer than four years had three or more placements. Likewise in the United Kingdom, Smith, Stormshak, Chamberlain, & Bridges Whaley (2001) reported that during any 12-month period, 50% of children in foster care disrupt their placements. These problems themselves then may contribute to future placement breakdown. Against this background, any theoretical understanding that can contribute toward stabilizing placements must be helpful.

I have observed that there are a small but significant number of children within the care system who present as unable to use resources available to them. They make individuals involved with them feel inadequate and useless. Even as toddlers, they experience repeated placement breakdown and readily become stigmatized by the system. For this group of children, care plans can be seen to shift from looking for an adoptive placement, to labeling a child as unadoptable, and finally as unsuitable for fostering. Frequently, this results in the child being placed in a children's home. The outcomes for these children are poor in terms of education (McAuley et al., 2006), attachment, and mental health (Meltzer et al., 2004), and create a disproportionate cost to society (Teggart, 2006).

In this paper, case material from work with two different children is provided. In the first piece of clinical material I describe my countertransference feelings and enactment before I had come to use "dead mother syndrome" as a theoretical framework. I then introduce the theory, taking a developmental perspective, which looks first at the emergence of object relations during normal development and goes on to contrast this with the "dead mother" experience. In the second piece of clinical material, I discuss my work with Vicky and the way it is grounded in the theoretical framework of the dead mother syndrome. It clearly depicts some aspects of theory in the dynamics of our relationship. I also reflect both on how this framework of understanding can be used to promote a sense of aliveness in individual work and also how it can help support the network around the child, with particular reference to the foster carers.

THE WORK SETTING

I work in a government-funded multidisciplinary and multiagency team that specializes in working with children in the care team. Our funding and team members come from social services, health (National Health Service), and education. The following disciplines are represented in the team: forensic child psychiatry, social work, clinical psychology, educational psychology, art therapy, and child psychotherapy. Since only one member of the team has a full-time post, we have to work very hard at communicating with each other.

MORE ABOUT PAUL

Paul was a 12-year-old boy with learning difficulties. I saw Paul once weekly for a period of 18 months. He came into care at age 9 due to neglect and was referred to our team two years later when he was on his third placement and that placement was also at risk of disruption. His carer complained that she did not feel as if she was a real person to Paul. She reported that whatever she did or said, it did not seem to ever be good enough or have any sense of value to Paul. Like his carer, I felt as if I did not matter to Paul.

Having completed his proprietary stroll around the room, Paul would usually settle down to play either with the sand or with the paints (seemingly without any interest in whether or not I participated). In the sand tray, Paul would bury dolls and cars. Not satisfied with just hiding these items, he would pile mounds of sand on top. When he was satisfied that these items were "dead and buried," he would repeat the whole process again in a way that I later understood to symbolically represent the repeated renewal of his internal object.[1] (An internal object can be thought of as being similar to an internal representation of an external figure, but rather than being an exact copy, involves a combination of both internal aspects of the self and external factors.) This activity was accompanied by a seamless commentary about what he was doing. During this commentary, he would make no reference to me. The burying seemed to symbolize exclusion from both internal and external stimuli. Like his carer, I too felt excluded from any relationship with Paul.

At the sink, Paul would conduct experiments with the paint. His experiments entailed repeatedly filling beakers with water to which he would add tiny amounts of paint and then pour the mixture away. These experiments were also accompanied by a rhythmical chanting commentary of what he was doing. For me, the sessions began to feel like a punishment whereby I was forbidden to participate in a scenario but was condemned to watch. I felt unable to form any meaningful relationship with Paul, and I could not see what effect my presence; (if any) was having on him. His carer too did not observe any change as a result of therapy, even though Paul reportedly enjoyed coming.

After several months of this repeated pattern, I found myself dreading our sessions. I would constantly be clock watching and willing the second hand to move faster. I even found myself silently repeating my own meditation mantra in parallel with his chanting. Perhaps I was mirroring Paul's experience of feeling that I had only myself to talk to. Alternatively, I might have out of conscious awareness slipped into an encapsulated aspect of myself as an attempt to keep alive.

In trying to understand the process behind my dissociation and resultant impasse, I began to wonder about what embodied memories were being kindled for me out of my conscious awareness. According to Stern (2003), embodied reactions precede our verbal responses within the transference/countertransference relationship. He suggests that "perception and action, like content and process, each play a role in creating the other" (p. 10). I wondered what it was that I perceived that prevented me from talking and also numbed my ability to think. What was I dissociating from?

Bromberg (2010) discusses enactment as being a form of repetition compulsion in which the patient needs the analyst to experience a sense of failing, in the same way that his primary carer failed him. He suggests that when the analyst comes up against uncomfortable feelings, it can lead to dissociation in that aspect of the relationship that is causing the problem. As a defense against this, the analyst may attempt to manage the relationship as a substitute for participating in it, and this results in enactment. I certainly felt a failure and wanted to gain control over Paul and how he used the sessions as a way of avoiding my uncomfortable feelings: we were involved in an ongoing enactment.

Pondering on the ways in which Paul's primary carer had failed him, I began to link the theoretical underpinnings of the dead mother syndrome with both Bion's (1962) concept of the newborn, living in the immediate present with no object constancy, and Winnicott's idea of object usage (1969).

A SELECTIVE OVERVIEW OF THE EMERGENCE OF OBJECT RELATIONS DURING NORMAL DEVELOPMENT

Bion (1962) suggested that infants are born without an internal space so that the infant's world is one in which everything occurs in the immediate present, with no intentionality or distinction between subject and object. According to Bion, it is through the continuous series of one-dimensional events in an immediate present that, out of conscious awareness, the infant's preconception meets with the object, thus enabling perception to arise. Bion (1962) linked frustration with the process of thinking and learning. He contends that it is only because of the mother's normal delayed response to meet her infant's needs that the baby becomes aware of the (m)other and thus starts the process through which first thoughts arise. In 1963, Bion introduced the concept of container-contained, in which he proposed that the infant develops an internal space via interaction with an object (internal representation) that is able to contain and transform the infant's poisonous projections. Through the introjection of and identification with such a containing object, he suggests that the infant receives the capacity to start the process of developing an internal space, itself capable of containment. Bick (1968) extended this concept, focusing on the feeding experience as being a precursor to introjection. She hypothesized that the concept of a containing object derives from the experience of the mouth closing around the nipple and that it is this action that is the first symbolization of introjection.

Since the 1960s, many developmental models have been proposed and the influence of the early intersubjective experience on the development of both internal and external reality is now widely recognized. Fonagy and Target (2007), along with Lyons-Ruth (1999), focus on the importance of maternal/infant gaze as a process through which meaning is derived from experience. Fonagy and Target (2007, p. 4) refer to eye contact as an "evolutionarily prepared mechanism" to enable shared consciousness. Knox (2004) and Wilkinson (2010, 2006), among others, describe how mind and meaning originate from within the process of interpersonal experience via such processes as contingent interaction. Schore (2003), Bromberg (2006), and others write about the connection between the quality of the intersubjective relationship and the capacity of the infant to develop his or her own ability to regulate affect. In recent years, there has also been research that suggests that brain structure and function is also influenced by the intersubjective experience.

From an object relation's perspective of development, a pivotal concept is that of psychic equivalence, referred to by Fonagy and Target (2007) to describe a developmentally primitive belief system in which infants believe that what they know, their mothers know. Likewise, what their mothers know, they know. In this way, knowledge is shared in what might be conceptualized as an intersubjective cocoon in which each participant knows what the other knows and that is all there is to know. This concept is related both to Bion's understanding of the infant functioning in the immediate present (before the development of an internal space) and Winnicott's theory of object usage (1969).

Emanuel (2012) reminds us that, according to Bion, the first thought arises from the felt, absent object, the "no thing." He cites the following from Bion: "Sooner or later the wanted (good) breast is felt as an idea of a breast missing and not a bad breast present . . . If there is no 'thing,' is 'no thing' a thought and is it by virtue of the fact that there is 'no thing' that one recognizes that 'it' must be a thought?" (Bion, 1962, p. 35). Emanuel then goes on to say that "The person has to be able to tolerate the experience of frustration caused by the absence of an object long enough for him to discover what it is that is absent. If the frustration is so intolerable, the no-thing experience is evaded, as the *absent* object becomes the *present* persecutor, which has to be evacuated" (Bion, 1962).

Winnicott (1969) proposed that, in normal development, the infant moves toward object relating, a process in which the object becomes meaningful. He distinguishes object relating from object usage stating that achievement of object usage requires that the infant first needs to recognize the object as an entity in its own right. This involves the infant placing the object outside of the self; in so doing, the original object is destroyed. When things go well enough, the object survives destruction by the infant. The act of surviving (without retaliation) imbues the object with a different value for the infant. The infant now has the possibility of communicating with and using the object. Winnicott suggests that the loved and hated object is continually recreated.

It therefore follows that if the predominant belief system is psychic equivalence, which infers no object usage, the infant will never be at risk of his/her love being unrequited. Under good enough conditions, the infant only gradually becomes aware that the mother is an other and the position of dependency can gradually be tolerated before opening up to a triangular relationship and Oedipal conflict. Instead, the absent but good object (Bion, 1962), by letting the child know he/she is loved, facilitates the child being able to tolerate small absences.

For the infant who has a preoccupied dead mother, the intersubjective experience will be very different.

THE DEAD MOTHER EXPERIENCE

Green (1986) portrayed the situation in which the mother is not actually dead but rather is preoccupied to the extent that she is not available to the infant and is consequently experienced *as if dead.* He introduced the term "dead mother syndrome" to summarize this situation. He describes a category of patient as blank or empty, for whom there has been an absence in psychic experience. He suggests that these patients engage in "blank mourning," a condition arising from the infant's mother withdrawing emotionally and being preoccupied to the extent that she is unavailable to the infant. He suggests that the infant is then faced with having to identify with an absent, emotionless mother. Green went on to describe how the infant's subjective experience of this relationship is devastating and "carries in its wake beside the loss of love, the loss of meaning" (p. 150). This loss of meaning and absence is then manifested in the transference/countertransference experience. (Alvarez, 2012, describes this in terms of a deficit or impairment of the internal object.)

Previously, I referred to meaning making occurring via such processes as contingent interaction. Clearly, with a preoccupied mother, the opportunity for contingent interaction and consequently making meaning of experience will be limited. This can be conceptualized in terms the failure of preconceptions to meet with realization (Bion, 1965). Stern (1998) equates such a situation with the child feeling as if he/she does not have a right to an inner life or to develop as a person. Rose (2011) suggested that a child parented by "an as if dead mother" is prematurely presented with an Oedipal, triangular relationship created by the mother's preoccupation.

Green suggests that as a defense against the loss of what is absent, the infant fills the empty space with a cruel object through the process of identification with the "dead mother." This involves a reinvestment of emotion. I imagine the internalization of a neglectful mother would increase the likelihood of persecutory feelings, and perhaps this is why the new object is described as being "cruel."

Rose (2011) emphasizes the fact that this replacement object is being re-stimulated and constantly recreated. He introduces the term *virtual object* to draw our attention to the fact that this recreated object now reflects something of the patient and is not simply an internalized representation of the mother. He emphasizes the point that this *virtual object* is omnipotently and continually being recreated as a way of exerting control over the relational trauma. I would add that, because for the child everything occurs in what Bion would call the immediate present, every new experience, every new moment, the object is recreated. The re-creation of a virtual object could then be regarded as a normal developmental process, which only becomes significant when attainment of object constancy cannot be achieved. Rose continues by reflecting that the purpose of the virtual object is to bring the trauma of loss: ". . . under the child's ego-control and subject to secondary process" (p. 207).

Green makes a distinction between absence and emptiness. He states that absence involves a lack, but unlike emptiness, absence promises the hope of fulfillment. My understanding is that emptiness does not require a past, whereas absence infers something once existed and could exist again. Absence, in contrast to emptiness, allows for the establishment of what Winnicott described as potential space, that is, a transitional or intermediary realm of mutual experiencing that lies between fantasy and reality. It is linked to the capacity to symbolize and I believe is a precondition for the development of object relations. This potential space may originate in utero through the mother's fantasies. Research on the influence of in utero hormones demonstrates that maternal stress compromises the normal regulation of hormonal activity during pregnancy and raises free circulating corticotrophin-releasing hormones (CRH) that mediate the effects of psychosocial stress on fetal development and birth outcome. Excess CRH and other hormones such as cortisol that pass through the placenta are thought to precipitate preterm labor, reduce birth weight, and slow growth rate in prenatally stressed infants. These changes are thought to arise due to inhibition of their receptors in the fetal limbic system and results in the impairment of the feedback regulation of the hypothalamic-pituitary adrenal (HPA) axis in infancy and adulthood. Weinstock (2005), Schore (2001), and Porges (2009) describe the link between a dysregulated HPA system and chronic dissociation. I imagine that such impaired regulation of the HPA axis would also impact the infant's ability to internalize an object.

Modell (1999) reminds us that the dead mother syndrome is a relatively rare occurrence, which involves a primary identification with an emotionally dead mother. This results in the child being unable to grow. Modell describes how the child feels as though it is not entitled to an inner life of its own — to become a person in its own right.

INTERNAL EXPERIENCE REPLICATED BY EXTERNAL EXPERIENCE

All children who enter the care system experience the very real, external loss of their birth family. A proportion of these children will also have had the subjective experience of being parented by a primary carer who is perceived as if dead by the child. As a result, the child too becomes affectively dead. Green termed this dynamic the dead mother syndrome. I propose that such early subjective experience in interaction with the actual loss of their mother may be a factor in the generation of repeated placement breakdown.

Rose (2011) describes how in the counter transference, these patients leave the therapist feeling impotent and deadened. It is therefore easy to imagine how such dynamics could be replicated and played out in the foster home and precipitate placement breakdown. I am acutely aware that I invested only an hour a week of my time. Despite my analytic understanding, I was tempted to rid myself of the narcissistic wound that I felt Paul inflicted on me. He made me feel useless and rejected. How much more vulnerable to similar feelings must foster carers be? They care for these children every hour of every day.

WORKING WITH THE TEAM AROUND THE CHILD IN ORDER TO SUPPORT THE PLACEMENT

The essential paradox for the foster families who care for these children is this: in order to develop future attachments and a sense of meaning, the child needs an "alive" responsive experience of parenting, but at least initially, these children are unable to tolerate such aliveness. I suggest that a child's initial experience of absence re-emerges in the relationships with his/her carers. Rose (2011) contends that in the analytic relationship, this experience re-emerges as desire so that nothing can ever be good enough. Furthermore, for the child in care, the *virtual object* that Rose describes as being "continually recreated out of the child's omnipotence" (p. 207) has the potential to be actually, bodily recreated by repeated placement breakdown. In terms of object usage, the object never gets the chance to survive destruction by the subject. In this way, the child never has to develop an attachment to an alive object and risk the danger that the object will leave.

The concept of the dead mother syndrome informs the support our team offers to foster families identified as caring for a child with this experience. Viewing a video of the still face experiment (Weinberg & Tronick, 1996; http://www.youtube.com/watch?v=apzXGEbZht0) has been found to provide a helpful context to discuss the importance of remaining persistently responsive to their foster child, even in the face of discouragement.

Both clinicians and carers find the experience of watching the infant trying to gain his mother's attention, a harrowing experience. Privately, individuals reflect both on how they were parented and how they have parented. Most people remain silent, taking some time to process their feelings. Taking the time to fully register the impact of the absence of responsiveness is a new experience for most carers. Each individual carer has had a different experience of being parented and therefore reflects on the experience differently, although everyone has clearly been moved. We point out how it takes quite some time, even for the child with normal development videoed in the experiment, to be able to accept his mother's approaches and reattune after a short period of nonresponsiveness. We extrapolate as to how much more difficult this process might be for a child who anticipates an absence and may never have had an adequate opportunity to "try out" an emerging sense of self-agency. We reflect on how children who may never have had the experience of being heard and responded to may find it both easier and safer to project a persona that does not care rather than risk forming an attachment.

When it feels safe enough to do so, we also think with the family about how their wish to terminate a placement may at some levels be paralleling the child's difficulty and despair about ever being able to form an attachment.

Even when the past history of these children is known and understood by the team, in terms of the impact this may have on development and behavior, the team around the child easily finds itself creating a split between those who identify with the child and those who identify with the carers. Clearly, such splits are unhelpful and can precipitate a further disruption as uncomfortable feelings are acted upon instead of being processed and hopefully contained.

Without in any way diminishing the importance of co-work with both individual children and their foster carers, our team has also come to recognize the value of having a colleague whose sole function is to hold in mind the dynamics of network meetings and who can reflect on these dynamics free from the pull to identify with any individual, which comes from developing relationships with individuals. In this way, splits within the network can be reflected upon as opposed to acted upon.

THE DEAD MOTHER SYNDROME AND REFLECTIONS ON CLINICAL WORK WITH PAUL

Rose (2011) draws our attention to the fact that these children create *virtual objects* in an attempt to master absence and a sense of being nothing by converting the absence into a nothing object. When there is an object, there is also the possibility of a subject. According to Rose, if there is no actual live object, outside of the child's omnipotence to challenge the virtual object, it can only give temporary relief from the feeling of absence. A new virtual object is created to fill the new sense of absence and so the cycle continues.

Paul's case material clearly illustrates this phenomenon and how before I had a theoretical understanding of what might be going on, I was drawn into an enactment by my countertransference feelings. Not only did I experience his sense of nothingness, but also his cyclical recreation of a virtual object had the effect of making the therapy feel interminable and for the pace of time to drag. Reacting to the transference, I decathected from the analytic dyad. This was unhelpful and I suspect would have rekindled Paul's primary experience of absence, driving the cycle of *virtual object* creation to continue.

For me, the sense of despair was ever present. The sessions with Paul resonated with Rose's description of themes being worked to the point that they no longer have a sense or shape. Paul's commentary seemed to have little sense or shape until I came to understand it as substituting for a narrative. As a child born to an emotionally absent mother, he would have had little opportunity to develop an autobiographical narrative. Significantly, his commentary also remained in the present moment with no past and little reference to intentionality. Paul seemed to be stuck at a very early developmental phase.

Perhaps my repetition of my mantra was mirroring Paul's experience, that is, that I had only myself to talk to. Alternatively, I might have out of conscious awareness slipped into an encapsulated aspect of myself as an attempt to keep alive.

Bion contends that, ordinarily, naming and combining of phenomena is a prelude to meaning. However, in a mental state of Hallucinosis, he contends that ". . . the mental event is transformed into a sense impression and sense impressions in this domain do not have meaning: they provide pleasure or pain. . . . .Meaning is lost, . . ." (Bion, 1970, p. 37).

My preferred understanding of my repetition of my meditation mantra is that I became *thin skinned* and open to Paul's experience in the present moment transcending meaning making.

Our present moment was, as Rose (2011) reflects, being constantly recreated but as if in a vacuole, void of meaning and form. I began to think about how Paul was letting me know about how his life, all his experiences, had no meaning or form. Rose concludes that rather than understanding this repeated process of deconstruction as a defense against meaning making, or what Bion (1959) would term "attacks on linking," it is actually the process of deconstruction that provides the link to the infantile experience of nothingness. Music (2009, p. 43) points out that such children may not be ". . . attacking links, but rather their links have simply not developed and grown together." What Paul needed from his carer and me was for us to try to provide some meaning by being more responsive to him.

This shift in my understanding brought subtle changes to the dynamics of our work. In particular, I paid attention to my posture, my prosody, and general aliveness in our sessions. It also nudged me into thinking about how to help his carer understand the need to persist in being responsive to Paul. The first change in Paul that I noticed was the occasional introduction of metaphorical questions. Even though he would answer these himself, I felt they represented both an internal and external potential space for relatedness. Slowly in psychotherapy, Paul became less repetitious and more open to my interpretations. His carer too, reported that she felt more like she existed as a person for Paul, rather than just a useful extension of his body to serve his needs.

CASE MATERIAL: VICKY

Vicky had been sexually abused by her mother's partner and came into care at the age of 6. She was first referred to me when she was 8 years old, following her third placement breakdown. During the time that I worked with her, she had three further placements, one in foster care and a further two in different children's homes. Vicky refused to see me for a period of 18 months when she was moved to the first children's home. Throughout this period I had regular meetings with her social worker and other professionals, and I ensured that Vicky knew I was willing to see her again if she wanted. The first clinical vignette comes from a time when she was in foster care. The second vignette is from when Vicky was in the second of the two children's homes.

During the period of the first vignette, Vicky would often try to disappear from view. Frequently, she would come into the room, close the blinds, turn off the light, and squeeze her body into a space between the couch and end wall of the room, where she would sit with her head between her knees, behind a curtain of long hair. Sometimes she would have me cover her in a paper carapace so that she was literally hidden from view. I understood this as her way of letting me know about her feelings, rooted in infancy, of not being entitled to exist as a separate person in relation to another. During these sessions, I was filled to the brim with despair and a sense of futility. The following case material was not typical but was pivotal in my understanding and our relationship.

Vignette 1, age 10

Vicky came into the room and sat at the table. She stared out of the window and was silent. She made no reference to me, and I was aware of a sense of absence and also of anticipation. Vicky dipped a paintbrush into the red paint and absentmindedly started to rhythmically spread paint back and forth on paper. Still gazing out of the window, she started to speak. She lacked affect and seemed to be in a different time and/or place. She told me about a dream she had in which aliens had abducted her. She was in a spaceship with an alien. It was comfy and snug, but then suddenly she was doing a spacewalk. She was outside the space ship. Throughout her telling me about her dream, she continued to paint in what I imagine was a self-soothing rhythm. At this point, Vicky turned to me and asked, "Why did you kill me?" I remember being unable to make sense of this, but before I was able to consciously register much Vicky lurched toward me. I went to block her and our hands interlocked. In the interlocking of our hands, something changed. Vicky did not immediately pull away. Instead, she slid her palms against mine. As she slowly pulled away, I became aware of the stickiness of the paint between us. In this moment, I understood that the session was not about being killed; it was about survival at a very primitive level: "Where do I become me? Not part of you?"

Reflections

Even before Vicky started to recount her dream, I was aware both that I was experiencing a sense of absence and anticipation. I think these feelings fit well with Green's distinction between absence and emptiness. Vicky was letting me know about an absence but, also through my sense of anticipation, her hope for something else.

There are many different layers to Vicky's dream and numerous possible avenues for exploration. At one level, Vicky's dream seems to depict the developmental process of placing the object outside the self and being precipitated into a triangular Oedipal situation, the analytic third, being represented by the absence of the snug and comfy space capsule. In the dream, the object does not survive the process of being made external and instead retaliates and is perceived as a (psychic) murderer. Vicky then equated me with her murderer. As she lunged toward me and our hands interlocked, she was presented with an actual boundary that perhaps gave some shape to her experience. This was a meaningful moment in Vicky's therapy, which she often referred to throughout the remainder of our sessions together. Without an understanding of the dead mother syndrome, it is probable that I would not have so clearly realized the significance of our hands meeting. Instead of robustly surviving as an object that allowed for something different to arise, and thereby enabled her too to survive, the moment would have been lost.

VICKY: MORE CONTEXT

As our work progressed (through two further placements), Vicky became able to articulate her fear of relationships. By this time (age 14) she was using public transport to travel unaccompanied to our sessions. It can be difficult for any young person to be responsible for his or her own attendance at psychotherapy; however, for the child in a residential unit it is particularly difficult. These young people have to negotiate allowing themselves to be emotionally open and vulnerable one minute and then they have to cope with the harsh realities of dynamics with co-residents and multiple staff at the home. Somehow, Vicky continued to come. She would regularly grumble that there was no point in coming, remarking, "What's the point of talking? It doesn't change anything!" She would complain, "The lot of you only pretend to care." She would deride others, and me, protesting, "You are paid to do what you do, it's your jobs."

On one occasion when I felt like I was walking on eggshells and therefore carefully pacing what I said, Vicky berated me for talking in what she called a "professional" voice. She said, "It makes me feel sick! Why can't you talk normally, faster, *with feeling?* That way I might understand what you're getting at." It was only with the distance of writing up the session that I realized that when I spoke slowly, she perceived me as an absent object. Perhaps she felt like she fell through the gaps in my utterances, which may then have put her in touch with her fight for survival.

Vignette 2, age 15

Vicky had asked to see her independent reviewing officer (IRO)[2] and planned to ask to be moved from her residential home to a foster placement. She wanted to complain about the bullying at the children's home. This was our first session after she had met with her IRO. Vicky seemed hardly able to bring herself into the room. She was still wearing her pajamas beneath her hoody. She sat on the couch. After several moments of silence I asked her how her meeting with her IRO had gone. She shrugged her shoulders and commented that it had been a waste of time. She had been told that there were no foster carers available. Vicky contended that she knew that was not the case. It was just that nobody wanted her—why would anybody want someone like her? She then went on to tell me how a visit to her maternal grandmother (who she has not seen for seven years) had been organized, but she had decided not to go.

I wondered about the visit to her grandmother. I asked her to let me know a little about her grandmother and also wondered if now she regretted not going.

Vicky shrugged and then told me that her grandmother was old and not well.

After a short silence I added, "And you're frightened you will just be getting to know each other and then she will go and die." Vicky replied, "Yes, like everyone else." She went on to list all the losses she had had in the past 18 months: foster home, residential unit, and permanent exclusion from school.

Reflections

Rose (2011) goes on to discuss a patient of his whose mother was not only preoccupied when the client was a baby, but also later left the family. Rose contends that the mother's actual absence resulted in his patient's mind creating both a preoccupying and preoccupied mother. Children in care all have the experience of the actual loss of the mother. I feel that Vicky's case material clearly illustrates both her sense of absence and her preoccupation with her lost mother. Vicky had the insight to understand that she was unable to meet with her maternal grandmother for fear of losing her.

By the time of this second vignette, I think Vicky had some small experience with me of an object that could survive being destroyed, and she was beginning to be able to use me.

CONCLUSION

Children who as infants were parented by an unresponsive "as if dead mother" may fail to establish object constancy (Green, 1986). These children can feel compelled to continuously recreate their primary object. When such a child is also in foster care, there is the real possibility of re-creating this internal experience in the external world; that is, the primary carer can actually be repeatedly recreated through multiple placement disruption.

I have found the dead mother syndrome provides a useful theoretical framework for understanding the experience of this particular group of children in care.

Reference to this theoretical framework has been helpful both in reducing splits within the team around the child as well as enabling the foster carers to remain responsive even in the face of persistent discouragement from the child. In individual psychodynamic psychotherapy, using this framework has prevented my clients and me from becoming dead to each other. Instead, I have been able to remain curious. Together with the foster carers and other members of the network, this has been helpful in enabling my clients to take the first steps towards taking the risk of forming an attachment.

NOTES

1. Discussed further on page 353.
2. In the United Kingdom, since the Adoption and Children Act 2002, an Independent Reviewing Officer (IRO) must be appointed to participate in statutory reviews to ensure that a child whose interests had been protected during care proceedings by a Children's Guardian continue to have those interests protected once a care order has been made. It is the role of the IRO to ensure that the Local Authority in fulfilling its duties and functions takes a child's views into consideration.

REFERENCES

Alvarez, A. (2012). *The thinking heart. Three levels of psychoanalytic therapy with disturbed children*. London, England: Routledge.

Bick, E. (1968). The experience of the skin in early object-relations. *International Journal of Psycho-Analysis, 49*, 484–486.

Bion, W. R. (1959). Attacks on linking. *International Journal of Psycho-Analysis*, *40*, 308. [Reprinted in *Second Thoughts*, 1967]

Bion, W. R. (1962). *Learning from experience*. London, England: William Heinemann. [Reprinted in *Seven Servants*, 1977e]

Bion, W. R. (1963). Container-contained. In *Elements of psycho analysis*. London, England: William Heinemann.

Bion, W. (1965). *Transformations*. London, England: Heinemann.

Bion, W. R. (1970). *Attention and interpretation*. London, England: Heinemann. [Reprinted in *Seven Servants*, 1977e]

Bromberg, P. M. (2006). *Awakening the dreamer: Clinical journeys*. Hillsdale, NJ: Analytic Press.

Emanuel, R. (in press). An application of Bion's theory of thinking and transformations in hallucinosis. An experience of supervision with Dr. Donald Meltzer. *Journal of Child Psychotherapy*.

Fonagy, P., & Target, M. (2007). Playing with reality: IV. A theory of external reality rooted in intersubjectivity. *International Journal of Psycho-Analysis*, *88*, 917–937.

Green, A. (1986). The dead mother. In *On private madness*. London, England: Hogarth Press. [Reprinted 2005, Karnac Books]

Klein, M. (1958). On the development of mental functioning. *International Journal of Psychoanalysis*, *39*, 84–90.

Knox, J. (2004). From archetypes to reflective function. *Journal of Analytical Psychology*, *49*, 1–19.

Lyons-Ruth, K. (1999). The two-person unconscious. *Psychoanalytic Inquiry*, 19, 576–617.

McAuley, C., Pecora, P., & Rose, W. (Eds.). (2006). *Enhancing the wellbeing of children and families through effective intervention: International evidence for practice*. London: Jessica Kingsley Publishers.

Meltzer, H., Lader, D., Corbin, T., Goodman, R., & Ford, T. (2004). *The mental health of children looked after by local authorities in Wales*. London, England: Stationary Office.

Modell, A. H. (1999). The dead mother syndrome and the reconstruction of trauma. In G. Kohen (Ed.), *The dead mother: The work of Andre Green*. London, England: Routledge.

Music, G. (2011). *Nurturing natures: Attachment and children's emotional, sociocultural and brain development*. Hove, UK: Psychology Press.

Music, G. (2009). Neglecting neglect: Some thoughts about children who have lacked good input, and are 'undrawn' and unenjoyed.' *Journal of Child Psychotherapy*, 35, 142– 156.

Newton, R. R., Litrownik, A. J., & Landsverk, J. A. (2000). Children and youth in foster care: Disentangling the relationship between problem behaviors and number of placements. *Child Abuse and Neglect*, *24*, 1363–1374.

Porges, S. (2009, April). The polyvagal theory: New insights into adaptive reactions of the autonomic nervous system. *Cleveland Clinic Journal of Medicine*, 76, Suppl 2, S86– 90.

Rose, J. (2011). The presence of absence in the transference: Some clinical, counter-transference and meta-psychological implications. In J. Rose (Ed.), *Mapping psychic reality. Triangulation, communication and insight*. London, England: Karnac.

Schore, A. N. (2001). Effects of a secure attachment relationship on right brain development, affect regulation, and infant mental health. *Infant Mental Health Journal*, 22, 7–66.

Schore, A. (2003). *Affect dysregulation and disorders of the self*. New York, NY: W. W. Norton.

Smith, D. K., Stormshak, E., Chamberlain, P., & Bridges Whaley, R. (2001). Placement disruptions in treatment foster care. *Journal of Emotional and Behavioural Disorders*, 9, 171–186.

Stern, D. (2003). *Unformulated experience: From dissociation to imagination in psychoanalysis*. Hillsdale, NJ: The Analytic Press.

Stern, D. N. (1998). *The interpersonal world of the infant: A view from psychoanalysis and developmental psychology*. London, England: Karnac Books.

Teggart, T. (2006). The mental health needs of looked after children. In D. Iwaniec (Ed.), *The child's journey through care: Placement stability, care-planning, and achieving permanency*. Chichester, UK: John Wiley & Sons.

U.S. Department of Health and Human Services. (2005). Child welfare outcomes 2002: Annual report. Washington, DC: Administration for Children, Youth, and Families Children's Bureau. Retrieved from www.acf.hhs.gov/programs/cb/publications/cwo02/cwo02.pdf

Weinberg, M. K., & Tronick, E. Z. (1996). Infant affective reactions to the resumption of maternal interaction after the Still-Face. *Child Development*, *67*, 905–914.

Weinstock, M. (2005). The potential influence of maternal stress hormones on development and mental health of offspring. *Brain, Behavior, and Immunity*, *19*, 296–308.

Wilkinson, M. (2010). *Changing minds in therapy: Emotion, attachment, trauma and neurobiology*. New York, NY: W.W. Norton.

Wilkinson, M. (2006). *Coming into mind. The mind–brain relationship: A Jungian clinical perspective*. London, England: Routledge.

Winnicott, D. (1953). Transitional objects and transitional phenomena. *International Journal of Psychoanalysis, 34*, 89–97.

Winnicott, D. W. (1969). The use of an object. *International Journal of Psycho-Analysis, 50*, 711–716.

When the Lullaby is Missing: Healing from an Infancy in Foster Care

Amy L. Cooper

Infant-Parent Mental Health research and contemporary trauma-informed developmental theory have highlighted the critical co-regulatory functions of the early attachment process. It is well known that shared gaze awakens this process; however, what has been less explored is the role of the human voice in calming the body and informing optimal development. The ancient energetic practice of Qigong Sound Healing offers an important model for regulating emotional functioning. The discussion of its use in treatment with an adolescent, who was emotionally triggered by an infancy on the streets and in neglectful foster care, offers a potential model for the benefits of integrating traditional Chinese medicine's view of emotions and sound healing into psychotherapy.

Sound awakens not only our psyche but our biology as well. Consider that a mother's milk drips at the sound of her infant's cry, our heart races at the sound of a child's tumbling crash onto the floor, and our eyes tear upon first hearing the word mama. Sound transcribes a world and we tune in to see how it resonates within us (body, mind and soul).

INTRODUCTION

I sit now in my San Francisco living room, and the winter sky is partly foggy and partly clear — baby blue. The sky seems to mirror my own quandary in writing about the use of Qigong Sound Healing practice into my psychotherapy treatment to support the healing of an infancy spent in foster care.

The cosmology, or worldview, of the Chinese medicine system, and the ancient thought of Taoist Qigong which preceded it, is depicted so symbolically and nondualistically that everything one might draw on to ground the approach must include both fog and clarity, chaos and order.

Therefore the Master
acts without doing anything
and teaches without saying anything.
Things arise and she lets them come;

things disappear and she lets them go.
She has but doesn't possess,
acts but doesn't expect.
When her work is done, she forgets it.
That is why it lasts forever.

The original Taoist text, like the selection above from *Tao Te Ching*, written by Lao-Tzu and translated by Stephen Mitchell (1992), has a poetic voice and often, as in my case, is learned at the feet before a master who teaches by stories and philosophies that are often not written down. When they are, the potency of the telling becomes less than the whole of the experience.

I am consciously choosing to interweave a poetic voice in this article so as to convey what I have learned by studying Zhineng Qigong in the United States and China with World Qigong Master Mingtong Gu, and integrating dimensions of the tradition into my psychotherapy practice. By using metaphorical language, I hope to convey the quality of the paradigm and the ancient Taoist sensibility of integrating a nonlinear state of awareness. The language, at its best, will become like a hum where the words drift into the fullness of the rhythms, tone, and cadence within them. After all, wasn't the history of psychotherapy influenced by myth and the importance of symbolic representation and long periods of quiet introspection to heal?

I will begin this article by reviewing the literature on trauma as it relates to healing from early neglect and abuse and the use of mindfulness practices. I will then give an overview of some of the relevant dimensions of Chinese medicine's cosmology, which is very different from the Western medical view. I will try throughout to offer the perspective of Asian thought, not in an attempt to make it an evidenced based approach but more as a way to open our perspective to the whole person and potential of integrating another worldview and practice into the web of our work.

The idea of a whole person with physical, emotional, and soulful dimensions is similar to our own psychoanalytic tradition and yet is drawn out of a different cultural paradigm with different assumptions. True to nondualistic thinking, I will not try to prove that one is better, but only allow that they may coexist in a unique and as yet unexplored harmony.

I will review dimensions of sound healing and then end with the case of a teenage girl who spent her infancy in foster care and I'll describe how I used the Sound Healing Qigong practice in our treatment.

TRAUMA

Contemporary psychotherapy is increasingly integrating mindfulness practices into the locus of treatment methods. Neuroscientists are studying Tibetan Lamas' brains in a meditative state. They are confirming the powerful impact mindfulness practices can have on entraining a state of calm and deepening one's capacity to regulate strong emotional states such as fear, anger, and depression (Hansen & Mendius, 2007; Hansen, 2009). Also, out of the Buddhist and Taoist traditions arose a lesser-known form of meditative practice, Qigong Sound Healing, which we will discuss later in this article.[1]

The state of meditative awareness awakens our interpersonal capacities. Neuroscientist Dan Siegel (2007) suggests that mindfulness practice creates "interpersonal attunement," develops empathy with others, and "harnesses the social circuitry of the brain."

When these qualities of interpersonal attunement are present in infancy, they support the developing infant's capacity for self-regulation and become the template for future engagement in relationships. When they are absent, a developing child needs enriching experiences, which can compensate for some of the loss.

Meditation helps us to tap into this interpersonal social network to compensate for some of the missing experiences of development. When we are in the sensitive presence of another we are inexorably drawn into an intimate brain-to-brain linkup. This neural bridge lets us affect the brain — and the body — of everyone we interact with just as they do us. This ability "to know another from the inside out" accounts for the immediate, visceral sense of resonance that we experience in moments of connection and empathy (Cozolino, 2006, as cited in Dekoven-Fishbane, 2007, p. 202).

These three attributes of mindful awareness, increased compassion for oneself, empathy for others, and mind body awareness that promote choice, are especially important for traumatized individuals. Seized by flashbacks and triggers of trauma, these resources of interactive and self-regulation are not available and choice becomes limited by the myopic focus of fending off a real or perceived threat.

As van der Kolk (1994) describes, we are wired to respond to threat with a readiness for action or flight; the amygdala sends alarms throughout the body, stress hormones are released, and muscles are tensed for action. In the case of trauma, our response to threat is over-activated and we need help getting our body back into the optimal zone of arousal.

Given the value of meditation to awaken a sense of "choice" in relation to the autonomic response to traumatic triggers, we can now appreciate the comment about Qigong meditation by Dr Pang, Zhineng Qigong founder and doctor of Western and Traditional Chinese Medicine: "The use of the mind's intelligence to . . . uplift the consciousness of the practitioner from an automated condition to that of autonomous wisdom" (as cited by Gu, 2011, p. ii). This autonomous self is one who is available to move comfortably between the personal and the interpersonal effectively. Change and choice may be developed in a guided meditation that draws on interactive (psycho-biological) regulation, which "involves the ability to utilize relationships to mitigate breaches in the window of tolerance and to stimulate or calm oneself" (Ogden, 2003).

Porges, of the University of Chicago, well known for his contribution to the field of trauma and the poly vagral nervous system theory, has studied among other things, the significance of the vagus nerve in slowing our heart rate and enabling us to calm down and reengage. For decades, Porges has been researching the role of sound and the human voice. Interestingly, he notes, "the Social Engagement System regulates facial muscles, including the sphincter muscles around the eyes that promote social gaze and emotional expressivity, and middle ear muscles that enable the human voice to be extracted from background sounds. The neural mechanisms for emotional cueing via eye contact are shared with those needed to listen to the human voice" (Porges, 2011, p. 5).

The invitation through sound healing meditation into a state of harmony and an inter-subjective field of interconnection becomes an interesting paradigm shift for those who suffer from the limiting beliefs of developmental trauma. Their experience is often like 14-year-old Shauna, whose sense was that her own body was not to be trusted; after all, early in infancy she was homeless and could not protect herself from harm. Like all of us with significant unmet developmental needs, she can be triggered by misattunement and become unable to sense her interconnection with others or even imagine a welcoming environment.

One of the ways that the human voice uniquely entrains a state of calm is through the "phrasing of music, especially when singing, that results in short inhalations and extended durations of exhalations. Physiologically, breathing "gates" influence the myelinated vagus on the heart" (Porges, 2011, p. 9). Functionally, when we inhale, the influence of the vagus is attenuated and heart rate increases. In contrast, when we exhale, the influence of the vagus is increased and heart rate decreases. "This simple mechanical change in breathing increases the calming impact and health benefits of the myelinated vagus on our body" (Porges, 2011, p. 9). So in listening to and making shared chanting sounds an individual, like Shauna, can recover an innate biological capacity for tuning into an inter- and intra-personal world of safety and calm.

Later, we will explore how Zhineng Qigong's Sound Healing was integrated into Shauna's treatment to create consistency and repetitive experiences of nurture, which had been lacking in her early development.

ANCIENT TEACHINGS

Qigong has evolved over 5,000 years and grew out of the Taoist and Buddhist traditions of meditation as well as the study of the cosmology of the universe and of human anatomy. The system is based on a concept of energy medicine and conceptualizes illness as blocked energy and vitality as the free flow of energy. It is the origin of the Traditional Chinese Medicine of Acupuncture (TCM) (Yang, 1997, pp. 13–19).

The word "energy" or "Qi" itself is not simply "energy" as it is often translated. Ted Kaptchuk (2000), the Harvard trained medical doctor who also studied TCM describes it this way:

> Qi is the thread connecting all beings. Qi is the common denominator of all things from mineral to human. Qi allows any phenomena to maintain its cohesiveness, grow and transform into other forms. Qi is the fundamental quality of being and becoming.

The Chinese medicine system use of the concept of Qi is obviously complex and multifaceted as is the practice of Qigong itself. In this article, I will draw attention to one dimension of the cosmology, the template of emotional alchemy, which might be termed a Taoist psychology (Kaptchuk, 2000, p. 159).

The paradigm of emotional alchemy developed over many millennia by observing common emotions and their impact on physical symptoms and by observing the *Tao* or the way of the universe. The nature of all things in the universe is perceived as interdependent, and likewise emotions are seen as integrated within the physical and spiritual dimensions of human anatomy. The physical function of the organ system imitates an aspect of the emotional dimension that is associated with that organ system. So, for instance, the liver is the body's purification system and is the seat of anger in a state of disharmony and clarity in a state of harmony. The idea being that as we hold anger within our body we inhibit the body's purification system's ability to function optimally.

In the Qigong and TCM paradigm, elation is associated with the heart, fear with the kidneys, worry with the spleen, anger with the liver, and sadness and grief with the lungs. In a similar way in the West, we associate the heart with love and the gut with instinct, and know that when we are afraid our kidneys give out. We have seen this demonstrated when we have had a young client who amidst a state of fear needed to run to the bathroom quickly.

Each emotion is conceptualized as having a virtuous dimension as well as a stagnating one. So when the emotions are blocked or repressed they can cause illness and disharmony. When they flow harmoniously they have a virtuous dimension. In a disharmonious form they are chaotic or unstructured; in a harmonious form the energy takes on a new structure.

Worry, for instance, in its chaotic form, is overwhelming and debilitating but in its structured form allows one to envision new solutions to old problems. Similarly, anger is transformed with relaxation and inner harmony to become clarity and kind anger. All of the primary emotions are transformed in their own unique alchemy (Kaptchuk, 2000).

SOUND HEALING & PSYCHOTHERAPY

Before I speak about the Qigong practice of Sound Healing, I want to highlight the ways sound is already an intrinsic, though often unacknowledged, dimension of every treatment. Then, I will review how sound can support a state of calm and help to address the reverberations of trauma.

Consider that music and sound are intertwined with psychological processes impacting our affective response to the environment, the relational world and our capacity to soothe ourselves, as well as our ability to express our inner stirrings.

Reflect now on those moments of silence within a therapeutic conversation and recall how, as you sit more deeply in the absence of sound, a new thought emerges or in the awkward silence a flood of tears arises. There are times when you whisper to a baby and the mother in dyadic infant parent treatment; you may also note how the pauses help her let go of her racing thoughts and slow her pitch to a whispering hum. You may not be conscious of these moments. As you do become more conscious, you may discover that there is a meaningful way you are already using sound and tone and silence to forge connection and make room for new experiences of self and other.

Too, there are unique sounds you make in the treatment with a young child or infant, which convey a world of meaning, such as ***"uh oh"*** when a puzzle piece falls to the floor and you go to retrieve it. In this process, the sound conveys and we can sort out life's puzzles together. Or ***"oww"*** as you see a toddler bump his shin against the table's edge. The sound itself says, "I know how that feels, too." Or ***"ahh"*** as you notice a baby take a deep sigh and as you make the sound she re-engages. As you look to father, he is sighing in relief, too.

We all know how our mood and state can change when listening to music. The calming effect of music was, not surprisingly, also intuited by a Russian Count who commissioned Johan Sebastian Bach's *Goldberg Variations* to calm his insomnia. Like Bach, we may not know that very slow musical movements increase alpha states in the brain, but also like him, we sense clearly how certain music makes us move into different states of awareness.

The language of brain states is deciphered by a kind of measurement — an EEG, or electroencephalogram. These electromagnetic wave fields pulse at different rates. Some pulse slowly, some medium, some fast and some super fast, as shown below.

- **Delta** (0.5 – 4 HZ). Associated with deep levels of relaxation such as sleep.
- **Theta** (4 – 8HZ). Associated with tranquil states of awareness in which vivid internal imagery can often occur.

- **Alpha** (8 – 12 HZ). Relaxed nervous system, ideal for stress management, accelerated learning and mental imagery.
- **Beta** (12 – 30 HZ). Associated with waking/alert states of awareness k-complex (30 – 35HZ). Clarity and sudden states of integration, the "ah-ha experience."
- **Super high beta** (35 – 150 HZ). Psychodynamic states of awareness

Alpha and Theta are activated by sound healing and music therapy. Pure sound without language can stimulate a tranquil Theta state, which is a state of vision and dreams and internal awareness. For those who are hypervigilant, this state is often hard to achieve by themselves because they are too worried about external danger to relax inwardly. When music includes lyrics, an Alpha state emerges. In this state, we become relaxed and aware of both the internal and external world. Athletes often refer to this state as "the zone" (Kenyon, 2001).

Early infant practitioners, such as Bonnie Bainbridge Cohen (1994), have developed methods of working with infants and parents that protect this internal state of awareness so that infants, from the start, can learn to make use of internal calm for integration and rejuvenation. Those who, due to early trauma, missed out on the protected state of internal awareness, supported by a soothing environment and a parent's lullaby, may need a more guided experience to find a calm internal state.

The sound of the human voice without recognizable words awakens an important dimension of the human mind — the right brain. Whereas the left side of the brain looks for logical patterns, the right side looks for novelty and paradox, that part of us that does not speak but intuits. Positron Emission Tomography (PET) scans of the brain show that when the right brain hears sound and music without language, it gets activated. When exposed to words alone, the left side of the brain lights up. When we hear music with lyrics, both sides of the brain become activated.

The activation of the whole brain is significant in the case of those who have been traumatized, as research now indicates that they may be less likely to use their whole brain when processing intense triggers. When they are guided into an internal awareness, other dimensions of their processing become available to them and they can process the information of both sides of their brain as speech and narrative is integrated into the process. Then, they too can move into "the zone" where anything could be considered. The sounds in the Qigong Sound Healing practice were developed over centuries and lore has it that they evolved by listening to the sounds people made when they had pain in a particular organ system. Perhaps like Bach's movement for the Count, they observed what brought deep relaxation and healing from stress. Similar to the sounds we make to comfort baby and restore full breathing in the body after a disruption, the sounds help breath and energy flow more freely within the body.

THE SOUND HEALING PRACTICE

We listen to see what the world has to tell us. We make up one dimension of our knowing based on what we have heard in the past and another based on what we are hearing in the present moment. We listen to the tone, rhythm, and volume even without the words and their laden meaning. It is said that 80 percent of communication is nonverbal. I imagine the sound's vibrational tone and body tone are the significant source of communication. That tone is drawn, we might imagine, by how the energy flows or is blocked within our body and vocal chords. Sense how differently your body's tone changes in response to a cry of a baby or her giggles.

We say attunement is at the core of relationship, that active listening awakens a felt sense of knowing oneself, and being embraced in the unfolding presence of another. We emphasize less the act of hearing itself; the felt tone that resonates in the sinew of our bones like cold ice with the sound of a screech, the contracting of our heart with the harshness of the words "never again" at a funeral of a missed beloved or mother. When we hear a bird's song on a foggy lonely day, we might even reconsider giving up, in the hopes we could exist long enough to let it empty our gut of all its churning and open us to the bliss of a bird song emerging from a budding branch.

Like the sounds of water lapping at the pebbled shore and wind billowing across open desert sky, we hum like the universe within and around us. Eighty percent water, we swish and swirl and vibrate with the diverse sounds of our world. Leaves crinkling under a deer's foot, the big bang, a chorus singing "Halleluiah" — we are made of sound traveling across time and space and its memory informs us still. Sing to me and one world arises. Yell at me another. Leave me alone in a vacuum of silence, yet another. Or sit with me in a shared meditative state of silence; still another view emerges. I will organize my sense of self and becoming, based significantly on these verses, utterings and their absence.

THE QIGONG PARADIGM

Each of the sounds creates a resonance and vibration in the body, which like many traditions of spiritual music, entrains the body to a state of calm and the free flow of energy. Each organ has three sounds, which correspond to the physical emotional and spiritual attributes of the organ system. The first sound typically awakens a physical response in the area of the organ, the tone quality of the transmission of the sounds literally vibrates within the body and the organs, and from a TCM perspective, activates the subtle body to initiate the free flow of energy and the unblocking of emotional contraction or holding.

In Zhineng Qigong, the emotional alchemy is awakened by visualization, sound vibration, and meditation. Typically when people are guided into a relaxed state through the meditation and ancient sounds, they report moving into deep state of inner calm and feel a release of blocked emotions, as well as clarity about the emotional states arising or dissipating. It is a practice that can be done alone, awakening one's relationship with oneself or with others or guided by a therapist or healer.

The emotional alchemy of sound healing is multifaceted as it has a relational component of being a guided meditation, as well as a positive interpersonal view that the shared state of mediation itself is healing. In other words, we do not heal alone but in a loving relationship to one another and ourselves and in a loving environment. Love, as used here, is the sense of holding another with curiosity and high regard unconditionally.

Conditional thought posits an "if then" paradigm. Whereas, unconditional thought posits an open and curious stance to the value of whatever unfolds, activating deep neutrality or even a deep intention to accept the creative contribution of each arising experience. This is similar to psychoanalytic thought in that the neutrality deepens the process of healing. However, it is more expansive in that it opens to nonconceptual thought or experience, which may be described as the felt sensory or energetic experience before we construct language or meaning. This felt sense and opening to nonconceptual thinking in many Eastern traditions is considered to be the emergent moment of healing.

When we are truly open to any possibility and are not attached or averse to a particular outcome then healing can deepen. Bruce Lipton, a cell biologist and former professor at the University of Wisconsin Medical School, states:

> This new biology takes us from the belief that we are victims of our genes, that we are biochemical machines, that life is out of our control, into another reality, a reality where our thoughts, beliefs and mind control our genes, our behavior and the life we experience. (Lipton, 2008)

This epigenetic perspective can help us imagine the impact our worrying may have on our bodily and psychological well-being and the way a worry-free or meditative state could lessen the allostastic load and improve functioning.

INFANCY WITHOUT A SONG

When I first met Shauna, she was in elementary school. She had spent her infancy on the streets and in neglectful foster care. When I met her, she lacked internal balance and coordination. Her eyes would quickly dart around the room not focusing on any object. She spoke in a whisper and did not have a healthy appetite. She was engaged in a hypervigilant search for what was about to overwhelm her. Her frail body was overexcited by internal and external stimuli. She had been in trouble at school for making raucous sounds. She was like a little cat shivering in the corner and hissing sporadically, unable to organize its bodily response to the absence of threat.

We might imagine that since Shauna was born on the streets, more than likely she was tucked in a stroller separated from her mother's heart beat, the sound most familiar to her from her time in utero. Her lullaby would have been the sirens, the occasional screams of the streets and the sound of her mother searching for food in the garbage cans at night, unmediated by calming touch and soothing coos. Her experience of touch might have been a rough wool blanket covered over her face to protect her from the foggy, dusk sky. She might have been cuddled some but often handled with the urgency street life demands; picked up to stop her crying at times but more often disrupted simply to move out of the way. Her sense of taste was more than likely not first developed from mother's milk but formula, which would not have been warm enough to calm her body as it trickled down to her tummy. There would have been no toys hanging above her crib to draw her eye to their flowing rhythm. This was more than enough of a reason for her to be removed by Child Protective Services (CPS) and placed in a foster home where another type of neglect ensued.

Following her first months of life living on the streets, she spent her early years in many foster care settings including a group home where she was physically abused. The circumstances of her treatment would be unfathomable to me, had I not read the reports written by the social welfare system to portray her multiple removals and her abusive treatment. I have worked with her and her adoptive family at different junctures of their challenges. Early on, her physical body was underdeveloped, so I recommended, in addition to play therapy with me, that the family find activities that would help her develop physical strength and balance. Also, I worked with the family on her unique attachment needs and on advocacy at school to alleviate issues that arose regarding her over-excited states and occasional bullying.

ADOLESCENCE

Shauna is tall for 15, beautiful in that way that her eyes are deep and reflective and her strong cheekbones accentuate her facial features. She is also confident in her stride when her adolescent body is not pulled into a despondent curl away from the world.

She has a native intelligence that seems to draw from a well much deeper than her early neglect might foretell. Yet a part of her intelligence does seem to come from her keen hypervigilant observance of human behavior. Shauna no longer tracks from a place of "what will go wrong" and overwhelm but rather from that adolescent place of omnipotence that she already knows grownups may "screw up" and it will be her job to bring them back in line.

There is an underlying anxiety though that she desperately wants them to get it right and when they do, she knows the difference. For although she had years of being neglected, she has had many more years of being listened to and supported. She still struggles with not wanting to be blamed for getting angry about the failures of others and can impulsively lash out or shut down in response to a perceived injustice. It was at one of these junctures of explosive anger that she came back into treatment.

Now 15 and wishing for more autonomy, she was reluctant to "talk about" why everyone was so troubled by her behavior and most especially her occasional outburst of anger toward her coach at school. This was the first time that she refused to talk things out, as though to prove there was nothing to talk about. From her perspective the coach probably deserved what the school was calling an "unacceptable challenging of authority." Everyone from the coach to the principal to her parents had already tried "talking it out."

In a family session, she stated, with eyes half cast and body collapsed into the couch, "I'm not going to talk about it–to anyone–anymore!" Over the years, she and I had found alternative ways of moving through challenges, such as writing secret notes when she was not ready to tell and banging toy drums when she was angry and could not find the words.

So, when I said, "How would it be if you and I met for a month on our own, without your parents and you got to relax and talk if you want to and I taught you Sound Healing that I learned when I was away in China?" "Ok," she mumbled, looking at her parents to see if this was going to fly. "A lot of people fall into a deep state of relaxation and may not talk at all," I said and caught her smile out of the corner of my eye, "but the agitation can dissipate for awhile, and sometimes that makes it easier to sleep and rest and that can make a world of difference on how we see things and function." Looking to her parents with a shrug that communicated, I said, "I'm not saying we'll get to the bottom of this today but it could help overtime."

Her parents knew when they adopted Shauna that her early trauma was going to pop up throughout her development. Yet, of course, they had not imagined how it would feel to be with an overtired teenager who refused to speak to them or acknowledge all their support as the school kept calling and sending home write-ups. "Yeah, let's try. I'm out of ideas," her father said and looked at Shauna with that lovely gaze grownups give kids sometimes as if peering beyond their eyes to a place inside that says, "We're in this together."

THE LULLABY

All emotions are pure which gather you and lift you up; that emotion is impure which seizes only one side of your being and so distorts you. — Rilke

The technique of Qigong Sound Healing is simple and yet profoundly integrative. It begins by guiding clients into a relaxed meditative state by helping them imagine themselves relaxing into the earth as they lie down and rest. Then, they may be guided into a sense of interconnection with the universe as though merging into a state of oneness. This is amplified by the Zhineng Qigong idea of merging into a loving energy field that extends in all directions.

As Shauna lay on the pillows, beginning to relax, I could not help but associate the nightly rituals I had with my own daughter where I reaffirmed that the world was safe and that I would be thinking of her as she relaxed and slept. I even made up verses each night about how the rivers were flowing with her stories and carrying her love.

Although the paradigm is different and the idea of a Qi field is unfamiliar, the simple idea that you are not alone and the world is a safe and loving place seems to be at the core of what allows each of us to learn to relax. The idea of Qi takes on multifaceted meanings as well and can be sensed by individuals like a wind within the body or a magnetic charge or a lengthening or opening of the physical body.

As Shauna relaxed into a meditative state, I chanted the sounds for each of the organs, repeating each of the organ sounds three times. Gently, I integrated the narrative dimension of the emotional alchemy, eliciting images in her mind of the five elements associated with the organs and of the light emanating into her body. Finally, I spoke to the emotional dimension of the system, guiding her to release any worry and feel the calm in the moment, or release fear and awaken gentle caution like water flowing over a stone.

I sat nearby and sang and spoke gently. My own voice became a signifier that I was caring for her and watching over her, and that I was not trying to fix her but simply support her own growth and development. The relational field of therapy and the Qi field of a co-created inter-subjective experience unfolded within the practice.

Following a period of relaxation, we discussed what she experienced and how it related to things that were arising at home and at school. Shauna realized that sometimes she acted with anger toward her coach when he did not give everyone a chance. Once she understood how this triggered her, she was able to finally tell her parents directly what evoked her anger. She also realized how her anger could be used productively to change the way the team functioned.

The emotional alchemy template for processing emotions became significant because it revealed an emotional maturity, and capacity for insight that teachers and her parents had begun to doubt since her recent angry outbursts. Similar to insight oriented therapy, the meditation provided a way to reflect on her inner emotional states and gain mastery about both what was triggering them and what she could do about it.

The construct that each organ held a contracting and an expansive dimension provided a way for us to talk about her own experience of emotions. Also, it became a way for her to reflect on which aspect of her emotions were at play when things flowed smoothly for her, and which ones were operating when there were disruptions internally and externally.

In addition, it allowed her to become calm before processing intense emotional states, which helped on a neurological level for her to be available to process the information. Also, seeing the dynamic system of emotional regulation as energy flowing or energy blocked provided a way to normalize her feelings and honor her innate energetic capacity to change the flow of the emotions through sound meditation and reflection.

Playfully, we can see now how the ancient concept of emotional alchemy unfolds. In the process of Qigong Sound Healing the emotions were transformed symbolically and energetically.

Shauna moved from a state of unstructured anger to a state of clarity, which transformed her experience of herself and others.

CONCLUSION

Integrating the meditative and energetic practice of Qigong sound healing into psychotherapy with a young adolescent girl raised in foster care supported her reentry into therapy. This unfolded within a trusting therapeutic alliance built on developmental and trauma theory. Nonetheless what is significant is that it provided the bridge back into treatment at a vulnerable developmental stage. The method of using energetic sound meditation provided a way to avoid pathologizing the client or evoking resistance to revisiting the lasting impact of her early trauma. Her positive experience demonstrated that the meditative and sound healing practices were calming to her and improved her relationship with others. Finally, it became a diagnostic tool to assess her emotional intelligence and ability to self-regulate and make use of positive relational support. These are all significant gains given her extremely traumatizing early development and relational failures.

Perhaps Shauna's positive attribution is the best summary. "Can we do Qigong, next time I have difficulty with my parents?" she asked at the conclusion of the four sessions. With relief, her adoptive father said, "I'm so glad you're willing to work things out with us." So as difficulties have come up to talk over as a family in the proceeding months, we begin therapy with sound healing together and then in a calm state discuss life's challenges and opportunities.

So, you see why we say "hush" when the truth as it is sensed and heard by our little one alarms them. And "hush" again so as to evoke through the tone, our minds to imagine the truth as it may be. And "hush" again as the truth is reinventing itself in dream and reverie. And development requires that we never stop singing to and listening to one another.

Similarly the ancient sounds sing to our heart, our gut, and our mind. First awakening what dwells within, then calming to transform one tone of life into another, like thunder becoming rain, the pitter-patter lets us bloom anew.

NOTE

1. During the Tang Dynasty (581–907 AD) Sun Si Mao described the use of the six sounds, which Buddhist and Daoists had been using for some time to regulate qi flow (Yang, 1997, p. 12).

REFERENCES

Bainbridge, B. (1994). *Sensing, feeling, and action: The experiential anatomy of body mind centering*. Toronto, Canada: Contact Editions.

Cozolino, L. J. (2006). *The Neuroscience of relationships: Attachment and the developing social brain*. New York, NY: Norton.

Dekoven-Fishbane, M. (2007). Wired to connect: Neuroscience, relationships, and therapy. *Family Process*, *46*, 395–412.

Goleman, D. (1995). *Emotional intelligence*. New York, NY: Bantam Books.

Gu, M. (2011). *Wisdom healing (Zhineng) Qigong: Activate and embody wisdom and energy for health and happiness*. Petaluma, CA: Chi Center.

Hansen, R., & Mendius, R. (Eds.). (2007). Buddha's brain: The new neuroscience and the path of awakening, *Inquiring Mind, Science of Mind*, 24, 1.

Hansen, R. (2009). *Buddha's brain*. Oakland, CA: New Harbinger Publications.

Kaptchuk, T. (2000). *The web that has no weaver: Understanding Chinese medicine*. New York, NY: McGraw-Hill.

Kenyon, T. (2001). *Brain states*. Conway, AR: World Tree Press.

Lipton, B. (2008). *The wisdom of your cells*. Retrieved from http://www.brucelipton.com/wisdom-of-your-cells/the-wisdom-of-your-cells/

Ogden, P. (2003). *From neurons to neighborhoods*. Conference presentation at UCLA. Retrieved from http://healingresources.info/pdf/article_ogden1ppt.pd

Porges, S. W. (2011). Music therapy and trauma: Insights from the poly vagal theory. In K. Stewart (Ed.), *Symposium on music therapy & trauma: Bridging theory and clinical practice*. New York, NY: Satchnote Press.

Rilke, R. M. (1993). *Letters to a Young Poet* (M.D. Herter Norton, Trans.). New York, NY: W.W. Norton.

Siegel, D. J. (2007). *The mindful brain: Reflection and attunement in the cultivation of wellbeing* (pp. 42, 298, 347). New York, NY: Norton.

Schore, A. (2003). *Affect regulation and the repair of the self*. New York, NY: Norton.

Lao-Tzu. (1992). *Tao Te Ching* (S. Mitchell, Trans.). New York, NY: Harper Perennial.

van der Kolk, B. (1994). The body keeps the score: Memory and the evolving psychobiology of posttraumatic stress. *Harvard Review of Psychiatry*, *1*, 253–265.

Yang, J. (1997). *The roots of Chinese Qigong*. Wolfeboro, NH: YMAA Publication Center.

Relationship Violence and Teenage Parents

Ambra Born

Teenagers involved in a violent relationship are four to six times more likely to become pregnant than their nonvictim peers (Saewyc, Magee, & Pettingell, 2004). Though this is an area of growing concern and awareness, there remain large gaps in both the research and available supports for these victims of relationship violence. We do know that teen parents have an increased occurrence of past abuse and increased likelihood of becoming sexually active at both a younger age and with older men when compared with nonparenting teens. Within the context of these riskier sexual behaviors, teen parents experience a high likelihood of relationship violence. This type of emotionally, physically and/or sexually abusive relationship can have a tremendous negative impact on the teen parent, as well as increased negative outcomes for the children. Throughout this article, the impacts of abusive relationships on teen parents, their children, and the service providers who aim to intervene will be explored.

The ever-changing landscape of adolescence poses many challenges; these challenges may never be more evident than when a teenager becomes a parent and never more complicated than when this parent is the victim of relationship violence. Within the population of adolescent parents, it is well documented that rates of historical and current emotional, physical and sexual abuse are quite prevalent (Saewyc, Magee, & Pettingell, 2004; Hillis, Anda, Felitti, & Marchbanks, 2001; Noll, Shenk, & Putnam, 2009). Within this group, there is also a strong indication of Relationship Violence (RV), also known as Interpersonal Violence (IPV), Teen Dating Violence (TDV), and Domestic Violence (DV). In fact, teenagers involved in a violent relationship are four to six times more likely to become pregnant than their nonvictim peers (Saewyc et al., 2004). While studies have struggled to effectively tease apart accurate rates of RV among teen mothers, estimates are as high as 55 percent among teenage mothers (Center for Impact Research, 2000). While this type of emotionally, physically and/or sexually abusive relationship can have a tremendous negative impact on the teen parent, there are also increased negative outcomes for the children of teen parents involved in violent relationships (Terry-Humen, Manlove, & Moore, 2005; Silverman, Raj, Mucci, & Hathaway, 2001). Throughout this article, the impacts of abusive relationships on teen parents, their children, and the service providers who aim to intervene will be explored.

Over the past decade, the focus of domestic violence has drastically altered to recognize and include teen relationship violence. While this remains an understudied population, studies to date consistently find that violence in teen relationships (including emotional, verbal, psychological, physical, and sexual violence) is far more prevalent than once supposed. This article will briefly cover abuse as it pertains to teenagers and specifically to teen parents. In comparison to adult IPV, teen dating violence occurs in both similar and dissimilar manners. Similar to adult IPV research, there is wide variety in definitions of relationship violence and debates in the field regarding what constitutes perpetration. For example, one debate revolves around whether an adolescent who reports willingly entering into a sexual relationship with a significantly older individual should be considered the victim of statutory rape and therefore seen as a victim of sexual abuse. Such debates, coupled with the likelihood of underreporting, as is common in adult and teen relationship violence, lead to difficulty in determining accurate numbers of victims. To date, studies have reported overall rates of teen dating violence to be as low as 10 percent when more restrictive definitions of relationship violence are used (Black et al., 2011) and well over one-third of all adolescents when looking at a broader definition of relationship violence (Center for Impact Research, 2000). This difference between the estimates is most common when abuse is defined based only on severe physical violence versus the inclusion of emotional/psychological violence and more mild forms of physical violence (e.g., noninjury producing physical assaults). Furthermore, it is important to note that research on both teen parenting and domestic violence tends to focus on females; as a result, there is limited data or focus on male survivors or teen fathers.

According to the Teen Power and Control Wheel (Domestic Abuse Intervention Programs National Center on Domestic and Sexual Violence, n.d.), a widely used tool in working with survivors of teen dating violence, the following are areas in which perpetrators exert power and control over adolescent victims: peer pressure, anger/emotional abuse, isolation/exclusion, using social status, sexual coercion, intimidation, threats, and minimize/deny/blame. While these are appropriate areas of concern within teen dating violence, this wheel does not incorporate all areas of abusive power and control faced by teen parents. The Teen Dating Violence Technical Assistance Center (2009) identified the following as areas of concern specific to teen parents involved in a violent relationship: increased isolation, shame and embarrassment associated with being a teen parent, financial dependence on abusive partner, and fear of losing custody of the children (pp. 2–3). This provides a blend of the Teen Power and Control Wheel and The Adult Power and Control Wheel (Domestic Abuse Intervention Programs, n.d.), which offers the following components that are applicable to teen parents: Economic Abuse and Using the Children.

Given that teen parents are often faced with limited workforce skills and a need to continue attending educational classes, teen parents often have limited ability to financially support themselves and their child. The perpetrator's ability to incorporate the children in abuse tactics is also an important component of teen parent relationship violence. In teen parenting situations, teen parents may feel pressure from overarching societal beliefs that teenagers are unable to adequately parent, coupled with a perpetrator's potential to degrade victims and cause them to call into question their own ability to parent. These pressures can lead to internal fear and external threats of losing custody of their child. Additionally, as there may be other adults judging a teen's ability to parent (e.g., the teen's care givers, treatment providers, social service), teen parents may feel they have limited resources available to counteract the perpetrators abusive use of the children.

Within the research on teen dating violence, especially that related to teen parents, researchers have found that a common form of abuse lies in birth control sabotage. According to research conducted by the Center for Impact Research (2000), 51 percent of a sample of inner city Chicago parenting teens experienced either verbal or behavioral sabotage of birth control. These methods of sabotage included physically forcing the women to engage in sex without birth control or using verbal coercion to prevent the use of birth control. The likelihood of birth control sabotage increases as the age difference between the teen mother and father increases; specifically, teenage girls are more likely to encounter birth control sabotage when in an intimate relationship with an adult male (Center for Impact Research, 2000). Interestingly, Wiemann, Agurcia, Berenson, Volk, & Rickert (2000) found that teen mothers who reported physical violence perpetrated by their child's father also reported higher incidents of planned pregnancy.

Teen dating violence research has demonstrated a difference between teen and adult relationship violence in relation to the identified abuser. In adult relationship violence, males are most frequently cited as the perpetrator; however, in teen dating violence, some studies have found that adolescent females have been identified as perpetrating more physical violence. While this has been indicated across multiple studies (Hamby, Finkelhor, & Turner, 2012; Coker et al., 2000), when researchers further explore this discrepancy, adolescents consistently report that the severity of physical abuse is far greater when the male is the perpetrator of teen RV (Hamby et al., 2012). Additionally, male victims of teen dating physical violence are far less likely to report feelings of fear or any physical injuries. It is important to note that, in general, studies finding an increase in female aggression are often looking at relationships in which both partners are adolescents. Within the teen parenting dynamic, this is not always the case.

Unfortunately, the fathers of teen mother's children remain a severely understudied population. As a result, limited data are available on their demographics and influence over teen parenting outcomes. What has been found in past research indicates that, in addition to concerns about birth control sabotage, when the father is older, overall rates of physical and emotional violence also increase (Center for Impact Research, 2000). In this study specifically, one half of girls with boyfriends 18–25 years old and three quarters of the girls with boyfriends over the age of 26 were victims of relationship violence. While the age gap between parents decreases as the teen parent enters later stages of adolescence, one study found that at minimum, one quarter of all teen pregnancies (beginning at age 11) involve a father over the age of 21 (Taylor, Chavez, Adams, Chabra, & Shah, 1999). Ryan, Franzetta, Manlove, and Schelar (2008) also found an increase in likelihood of acquiring a sexually transmitted disease in young adulthood when a teenage female under the age of 16 has been sexually active with a partner at least three years older; this group was also at higher risk of teenage pregnancy. In the study by Ryan et al. (2008), researchers found that 10 percent of the sample had engaged in early sex with an older partner.

As adolescent mothers have an increased likelihood of intimate relationship involvement with adult males, the data on incidents of perpetration become more convoluted as teen dating violence studies often focus on relationships in which both partners are adolescents. In regard to teen parents, specifically mothers, research has shown that 50–80 percent of teen mothers have been victimized within the context of an intimate relationship, typically by their child's father (Leiderman & Almo, 2001). Part of the discrepancy between these numbers lies in the definition of RV versus child abuse, especially when the teenager becomes pregnant through incest or statutory rape; additional discrepancies are found when birth control sabotage and emotional abuse are included.

A study by Hamby et al. (2012) looked at the incidence of current RV as well as the historical incidence of abuse among respondents of the National Survey of Children's Exposure to Violence. Findings concluded that every adolescent who had been physically victimized in an intimate relationship also endorsed at least one other form of victimization. Among these, intimate partners were responsible for only 5 percent of these additional incidents of victimization. In this same study, 66 percent of the victims of physical teen dating violence had witnessed family member assault. While these family assaults were not broken down into specific types of incidents, it is clear that violence within the home leads to greater risks for the children. This finding becomes increasingly important when looking at prevention, intervention and at prognosis for children raised in a home with relationship violence.

When a teen parent enters into treatment, the reasons are often widely varied. Some may enter due to concerns raised about their parenting ability, others as a result of their own trauma history, and others related to various emotional or behavioral concerns unrelated to either being a parent or exposure to trauma. Regardless the reasons for seeking treatment, it is vital for providers to have a keen awareness of the needs and safety concerns of teen parents. Given that many of these teen parents have a history of abuse by their primary caregiver, and therefore limited or unhealthy levels of support from their family of origin, they are at increased likelihood (in comparison to teens without an abuse history) to be dependent on the father of their children for myriad means of support. Among other things, this may include housing, day care in order to continue attending school programs, food and clothing for the child and themselves, and emotional support. In relationship violence situations, the perpetrator has multiple areas in which the teen parent can be controlled and coerced. One area of great concern for both the teen parent and the child is the high potential for high school drop out on the part of the teen parent; this can be directly linked to multiple negative outcomes for both the teen parent and the child.

Teen parents demonstrate a higher than their peers risk for dropping out of school, which reduces their chances for current and future higher paying jobs and access to emotional and financial resources (Perper, Peterson, & Manlove, 2010). In addition, Mersky and Reynolds (2007) found that rates of teenage pregnancy are increased among individuals whose mothers did not complete high school. Given these findings, any treatment intervention with a teen parent should include supporting the completion of a high school diploma. As this impacts both preventing multigenerational teen pregnancy and providing better long-term options to teen parents, this is a vital component to success. Within the context of relationship violence, limiting access to school increases the teen parent's isolation and therefore dependence on the perpetrator. Given that this lack of education is directly linked to lower paying jobs and more limited resources, it is important that these adolescents are supported and encouraged by treatment providers.

Sussex and Corcoran (2005) highlighted the need to focus on rates of depression in adolescent parents, especially as it pertains to social isolation. It is well documented that children raised by parents suffering from depression demonstrate a great deal of negative outcomes, including worse physical health, insecure attachment, lower academic performance, and higher incidence of internalizing and externalizing mental illnesses (England & Sim, 2009). In addition, Cox et al. (2008) found a decrease in maternal parenting confidence among adolescent mothers suffering from depression. This, as well, was potentially moderated by social support. As RV and isolation are strongly linked, addressing this component of social connectedness is vital.

It is difficult to determine specific areas of concern for a child being raised by a parent involved in relationship violence because there is limited specific research available. What is known is that children raised around domestic violence are more likely to demonstrate emotional, physical, behavioral, and social impairments than children raised without violence in the home (Holt, Buckley, & Whelan, 2008). Studies have also shown that children demonstrate an increased likelihood of entering into a violent intimate relationship themselves if they have experienced emotional abuse, physical abuse or neglect by a caregiver, have been sexually assaulted, or have witnessed violence in the home (Wekerle et al., 2009; Jouriles, Mueller, Rosenfield, McDonald, & Dodson, 2012; Hamby et al., 2012). Additionally, of children who witness violence in the home, approximately 56 percent have reported at least one additional occurrence of maltreatment in adolescence or adulthood (Hamby, Finkelhor, Turner, & Ormrod, 2010).

Research on children born to teen mothers has found that there may be areas in which these children fall behind their peers. One longitudinal study found that 72 percent of children born to teen mothers often demonstrate developmental delay in at least one area by the age of 3 (Whitman, Borkowski, Keogh, & Weed, 2001). Another study found that children of teen parents (younger than 17 years of age) are more likely to have lower "reading, math, and general knowledge test scores and lower proficiencies on both reading and math assessments" at the start of kindergarten (Terry-Humen et al., 2005, p. 15). This same study also found a higher likelihood of some negative behaviors, a decrease in some positive behaviors, and lower fine motor skills in children born to mothers under the age of 17. It is important to note that when this study controlled for maternal, child, and/or family characteristics, many of these delays were less evident. In fact, in one positive area, that of social interaction, children of mothers younger than 17 scored higher than those of mothers 22–29 years of age. This study highlights that while there does appear to be areas in which many teen parents may benefit from extra support, the larger issues are those of socioeconomic status and family structure (e.g., single family household). This can likely also be applied to households in which relationship violence is present.

Studies have also demonstrated that children born to teen mothers are at a higher risk of enduring child abuse (Afifi & Brownridge, 2008). George, Harden, and Lee (2008) found that in comparison to women who gave birth to their first child between the ages of 20 and 21, younger teen parents were more than twice as likely to have a child enter foster care. Additionally, they found that one in ten children born to young teen parents had a history of abuse or neglect reported to social services. Though neither of these studies looked specifically at teen parents who were victims of relationship violence, it appears plausible that for this population the rates of child abuse and neglect may be even higher.

Given that there are many ways in which a child and teen parent can be negatively affected by relationship violence, determining appropriate treatment strategies and interventions can be vital. As treatment providers working with teen parents, it is important that we honor the adolescent developmental needs and the needs of a survivor by empowering the teen parent to make their own informed decisions. Through the course of therapy, service providers are often faced with a multitude of obstacles when working with both adolescents and survivors of interpersonal violence. When these are combined, treatment providers are frequently left feeling helpless and overwhelmed by the many challenges faced on the client's road to health and well-being. Recognizing our own limitations and honoring the client's right to make his or her own decisions can be two of the most important components in our role as therapists. One aspect of this is recognizing and supporting the reasons why these teen parents continue to stay in a violent relationship.

Women have reported remaining with a violent partner for several reasons, including need for financial support, fear of losing custody of the children, increase in levels of violence when trying to leave, and societal pressures (Barnett, 2000; Barnett, 2001). When looking at the perceived relationship between adolescent partners, Giordano, Soto, Manning, and Longmore (2010) found that the perception of partner-caring, love, and intimate self-disclosure were similar between relationships displaying violence and those that do not report any violence. Interestingly, adolescents who reported higher levels of provision and receipt of instrumental benefits demonstrated significantly higher incidents of violence. This highlights the need to address the positive qualities of these relationships and help teen parents learn to identify warning signs of violence. In part, this finding likely speaks to the greater level of dependence victims are often forced into when in a violent relationship. While this may appear to be an unhealthy level of dependence from a treatment provider's perspective, from inside the relationship, it appears that these higher levels of instrumental benefits may fill a need for greater levels of support and nurturing.

As adolescents and survivors of relationship violence are best able to make lasting changes when the decisions come from within themselves, treatment providers are often left watching clients reengage in violent relationships. In fact, on average, victims attempt to leave a violent relationship more than five times prior to successfully escaping (Barnett, 2000). While it can be easy for treatment providers to see the damaging impacts on our clients, it is ultimately up to the client to decide when to leave. Two important pieces in helping teenagers make this decision are proving knowledge and modeling healthy relationships.

Our role as treatment providers is often one of education. Given that many of these teen parents have a history of abuse by their caregivers, part of the role of a therapist is to not only demonstrate through the therapist-client interaction what constitutes a healthy relationship, but also to have open dialogue around what violence looks like and what healthy love looks like in the context of an intimate relationship. Distributed by the National Center on Domestic and Sexual Violence (Domestic Abuse Intervention Programs & National Center on Domestic and Sexual Violence, n.d.), the Teen Equality Wheel defines healthy relationships as containing: Negotiation and Fairness; Nonthreatening Behavior; Communication; Shared Power; Self-Confidence and Personal Growth; Honesty and Accountability; Trust and Support; and Respect. Applicable areas on the Adult Equality Wheel (Domestic Abuse Intervention Programs & National Center on Domestic and Sexual Violence, n.d.) include Economic Partnership; Shared Responsibility; and Responsible Parenting. As we help a teen parent redefine how healthy love can look and feel, this can also help them create a healthier relationship with their child.

A study by Maas, Fleming, Herrenkohl, and Catalano (2010) found that bonding to parents served as a protective factor against teen dating violence, as bonding reduced likelihood of substance use in adolescent females and early adolescent externalizing behaviors in males (both of which have links to increased levels of involvement in relationship violence). As the impacts of RV on the parent-child attachment can be negatively affected due to the increased intimate partner demands placed on the victim, helping the teen parent learn healthy ways to bond with his or her child can serve as a protective factor for later victimization of the child as well as provide increased confidence for the parent. As many of these teen parents have abusive or neglectful families of origin, the therapeutic relationship can become a source of redefining a healthy relationship. Through this experience, teen parents can learn new ways to engage with themselves and their child, providing a better chance for success.

While there are vital ways a therapeutic relationship can benefit a teen parent, there are challenges faced by treatment providers. In addition to frustration around watching a teen parent make potentially unhealthy decisions within the violent relationship, there are also legal responsibilities and overall feelings of burnout. One challenging aspect of teen parent relationship violence lies in mandatory reporting. While most states are consistent in stating that violence occurring in front of children is a mandated reporting issue, relationship violence involving a teenager becomes more complicated. As the teen parent is often also a minor, there can be an expectation of mandated reporting, especially when the perpetrator (in this case, the father of the baby) is an adult. Additionally, when the parent of the teenager is aware of teen dating violence, there may also be a need to report this potential neglect to authorities. It is important for all providers to check their local laws around reporting relationship violence with teens.

As teen parents straddle the adolescent and the adult worlds, it is vital that we both meet them where they are at in adolescent development and support them in their adult role of being a parent. Given that rates of teen relationship violence are extraordinarily high, it is vital that issues of healthy teen dating are incorporated in almost any teen parent's treatment plan. Additionally, with the extremely high likelihood of historical abuse, especially abuse perpetrated by his or her own caregivers, it is important to help these teen parents experience a healthy, safe relationship. Through providing teen parents with knowledge and positive interpersonal experiences, we can empower these young parents and their children in finding greater success and well-being.

REFERENCES

Afifi, T. O., & Brownridge, D. A. (2008). Physical abuse of children born to adolescent mothers: The continuation of the relationship into adult motherhood and the role of identity. In T. I. Richardson & M. V. Williams (Eds.), *Child abuse and violence* (pp. 19–42). Hauppauge, NY: Nova Science Publishers.

Barnett, O. W. (2000). Why battered women do not leave, part 1: External inhibiting factors within society. *Trauma Violence Abuse*, *1*(4), 343–372.

Barnett, O. W. (2001). Why battered women do not leave, part 2: External inhibiting factors —social support and internal inhibiting factors. *Trauma Violence Abuse*, *2*(1), 3–35.

Black, M. C., Basile, K. C., Breiding, M. J., Smith, S. G., Walters, M. L., Merrick, M. T., . . . Stevens, M. R. (2011). The National Intimate Partner and Sexual Violence Survey (NISVS): 2010 summary report. Atlanta, GA: National Center for Injury Prevention and Control, Centers for Disease Control and Prevention.

Center for Impact Research. (2000). Domestic violence and birth control sabotage: A report from the Teen Parent Project. Chicago, IL: Center for Impact Research.

Coker, A. L., McKeown, R. E., Sanderson, M., Davis, K. E., Valois, R. F., & Huebner, E. S. (2000). Severe dating violence and quality of life among South Carolina high school students. *American Journal of Preventive Medicine*, *19*, 220–227.

Cox, J. E., Buman, M., Valenzuela, J., Joseph, N. P., Mitchell, A., & Woods, E. R. (2008). Depression, parenting attributes, and social support among adolescent mothers attending a teen tot program. *Journal of Pediatric Adolescent Gynecology*, *21*(5), 275–281.

Domestic Abuse Intervention Programs. (n.d.). Adult equality wheel. Retrieved from http://www.ncdsv.org/publications_wheel.html

Domestic Abuse Intervention Programs. (n.d.). Adult power and control wheel. Retrieved from http://www.ncdsv.org/publications_wheel.html

Domestic Abuse Intervention Programs & National Center on Domestic and Sexual Violence (n.d.). Teen equality wheel. Retrieved from http://www.ncdsv.org/publications_wheel.html

Domestic Abuse Intervention Programs & National Center on Domestic and Sexual Violence (n.d.). Teen power and control wheel. Retrieved from http://www.ncdsv.org/publications_wheel.html

England, M. J., & Sim, L. J. (Eds.). (2009). Depression in parents, parenting, and children: Opportunities to improve identification, treatment, and prevention. Washington, DC: The National Academies Press.

George, R. M., Harden, A. W., & Lee, B. J. (2008). Effects of early childbearing on child maltreatment and placement in foster care. In S. Hoffman & R. Maynard (Eds.), *Kids having kids: Economic costs and social consequences of teen pregnancy* (pp. 257–288). Washington, DC: Urban Institute.

Giordano, P. C., Soto, D. A., Manning, W. D., & Longmore, M. A. (2010). The characteristics of romantic relationships associated with teen dating violence. *Social Science Research*, *39*, 863–874.

Hamby, S., Finkelhor, D., & Turner, H. (2012). Teen dating violence: Co-occurrence with other victimizations in the national survey of children's exposure to violence. *Psychology of Violence*, *2*(2), 111–124.

Hamby, S., Finkelhor, D., Turner, H., & Ormrod, R. (2010). The overlap of witnessing partner violence with child maltreatment and other victimizations in a nationally representative survey of youth. *Child Abuse & Neglect*, *34*, 734–741.

Hillis, S. D., Anda, R. F., Felitti, V. J., & Marchbanks, P. A. (2001). Adverse childhood experiences and sexual risk behavior in women: A retrospective cohort study. *Family Planning Perspectives*, *33*(5), 206–211.

Holt, S., Buckley, H., & Whelan, S. (2008). The impact of exposure to domestic violence on children and young people: A review of the literature. *Child Abuse & Neglect*, *32*(8), 797–810.

Jouriles, E. N., Mueller, V., Rosenfield, D., McDonald, R., & Dodson, M. C. (2012). Teens' experiences of harsh parenting and exposure to severe intimate partner violence: Adding insult to injury in predicting teen dating violence. *Psychology of Violence*, *2*(2), 125–138.

Leiderman, S., & Almo, C. (2001). Interpersonal violence and teen pregnancy: Prevalence and implications for practice and policy. Washington, DC: Healthy Teen Network.

Maas, C. D., Fleming, C. B., Herrenkohl, T. I., & Catalano, R. F. (2010). Childhood predictors of teen dating violence victimization. *Violence and Victims*, *25*(2).

Mersky, J. P., & Reynolds, A. J. (2007). Predictors of early childbearing: Evidence from the Chicago longitudinal study. *Children and Youth Services Review*, *29*(1), 35–52.

Noll, J. G., Shenk, C. E., & Putnam, K. T. (2009). Childhood sexual abuse and adolescent pregnancy: A meta-analytic update. *Journal of Pediatric Psychology*, *34*(4), 366–378.

Perper, K., Peterson, K., & Manlove, J. (2010). Diploma attainment among teen mothers [Fact sheet]. Retrieved from www.childtrends.org/.../child_trends-2010_01_22_FS_diplomaattainment. pdf

Ryan, S., Franzetta, K., Manlove, J. S., & Schelar, E. (2008). Older sexual partners during adolescence: Links to reproductive health outcomes in young adulthood. *Perspectives on Sexual and Reproductive Health*, *40*(1), 17–26.

Saewyc, E. M., Magee, L., & Pettingell, S. E. (2004). Teenage pregnancy and associated risk behaviors among sexually abused adolescents. *Perspectives on Sexual and Reproductive Health*, *36*(3), 98–105.

Silverman, J. G., Raj, A., Mucci, L. A., & Hathaway, J. E. (2001). Dating violence against adolescent girls and associated substance use, unhealthy weight control, sexual risk behavior, pregnancy, and suicidality. *Journal of the American Medical Association*, *286*(5), 572–579.

Sussex, B., & Corcoran, K. (2005). The impact of domestic violence on depression in teen mothers: Is the fear or threat of violence sufficient? *Brief Treatment and Crisis Intervention*, *5*, 109–120.

Taylor, D. J., Chavez, G. F., Adams, E. J., Chabra, A., & Shah, R. S. (1999). Demographic characteristics in adult paternity for first births to adolescents under 15 years of age. *Journal of Adolescent Health*, *24*(4), 251–258.

Teen Dating Violence Technical Assistance Center. (2009). Teen pregnancy, parenting, and dating violence (Brief No. 8). Retrieved from www.breakthecycle.org/pdf/ta-issue-brief-10-09.pdf

Terry-Humen, E., Manlove, J., & Moore, K. A. (2005). *Playing catch-up: How children born to teen mothers fare*. The National Campaign to Prevent Teen Pregnancy. Retrieved from http://www.teenpregnancy.org/works/pdf/PlayingCatchUp.pdf

Wekerle, C., Leung, E., Wall, A. M., MacMillan, H., Boyle, M., Trocme, N., & Waechter, R. (2009). The contribution of childhood emotional abuse to teen dating violence among child protective services-involved youth. *Child Abuse and Neglect*, *33*, 45–58.

Whitman, T., Borkowski, J., Keogh, D., & Weed, K. (2001). *Interwoven lives: Adolescent mothers and their children*. Mahwah, NJ: Lawrence Erlbaum.

Widom, C. S., Czaja, S., & Dutton, M. A. (2008). Childhood victimization and lifetime revictimization. *Child Abuse and Neglect*, *32*, 785–796.

Wiemann, C. M., Agurcia, C. A., Berenson, A. B., Volk, R. J., & Rickert, V. I. (2000). Pregnant adolescents: Experiences and behaviors associated with physical assault by an intimate partner. *Maternal and Child Health Journal*, *4*(2), 93–101.

Fostering Healthy Attachment Between Substance Dependent Parents and Their Infant Children

June Madsen Clausen
Rosana M. Aguilar
Mark E. Ludwig

Infants of parents with substance abuse problems enter foster care at a higher rate than infants of nonabusing parents and are at a higher risk for attachment problems and child maltreatment. The current study evaluates the impact of a 10-week infant massage intervention designed to increase attachment between parents in a drug rehabilitation facility and their infants. The program focuses on parental awareness of infant's internal states, the development of skills for self-regulation of affect, the calming of their child, and the development of a capacity for sustained positive parent-child interaction so that parents can become more available in the psychological space and time they spend with their infant children. Parent participants, interviewed before and after the intervention, completed a demographic and program evaluation survey, as well as standardized measures of parent knowledge of child development, parenting stress, and depression. Results indicate trends towards decreased parental stress, increased knowledge of good parenting practices, better relatedness between parent and infant, and improved parenting self-efficacy, suggesting that attachment interventions with substance dependent parents may have substantial benefits for the parent-child relationship as well as the mental health functioning of parent and child.

BACKGROUND

Child abuse and neglect is an enormous social problem with staggering emotional, developmental, educational, and financial costs to individuals, families, and communities (Briggs, Thompson, Ostrowski, & Lekwauwa, 2011; Frederico, Jackson, & Black, 2008; Paolucci, Genuis, & Violato,

2001; Walsh, Dawson, & Mattingly, 2010; Zielinski, 2009). Without parents who modeled good parenting and without effective intervention by communities and mental health professionals, many children who are abused and neglected grow up to be abusive and neglectful parents who perpetuate the devastation into which they were born (Dixon, Browne, & Hamilton-Giachritsis, 2009; Fang & Corso, 2007; Fraiberg, Adelson, & Shapiro, 1975; Schwerdtfeger & Goff, 2007). One of the most common pathways for intergenerational transmission of abuse and neglect is substance abuse and dependence (Appleyard, Berlin, Rosanbalm, & Dodge, 2011).

Many children who are abused and neglected and who do not receive proper support and intervention become dependent on substances and unable to properly care for their own children (Appleyard et al., 2011; Dore & Doris, 1998; Kerwin, 2005; Lansford, Dodge, Pettit, & Bates, 2010). However, work with individuals who are substance dependent is difficult; research demonstrates that substance abuse treatment is often ineffective and relapse is common, particularly for individuals who also struggle with other psychiatric disorders, as is often true for individuals who experience abuse and neglect (Back, 2010; Berglund et al., 2003; Conway, Compton, Stinson, & Grant, 2006; McLellan, Lewis, O'Brien, & Kleber, 2000). Studies of parents in residential detoxification units reveal that three fourths (75.8 percent) have a history of previous admission to a substance abuse treatment center and 10 percent have three or more prior admissions (Redelinghuys & Dar, 2008).

Building a healthy and secure relationship with the primary caregiver is one of the infant's most important developmental milestones and maternal attunement is key in the development of secure attachment (Bowlby, 1969; Bruskas, 2010; Silver & Dicker, 2007; Slade, 2002). A lack of healthy attachment in infancy can lead to problematic stress management and develop into problematic behavior later in life (Bakermans-Kranenburg, Van Ijzendoorn, & Juffer, 2005; Schore, 1994). However, intervening with substance dependent parents who are in early stages of treatment for their addiction in order to improve their parenting and encourage the formation of healthy attachment with their infant children is enormously challenging.

Caregivers who are substance dependent have a difficult time forming healthy and secure attachment bonds with their children; substance dependent mothers are twice as likely as parents who are nonsubstance dependent to lose custody of their children due to repeated substance abuse and the neglect of their children (Suchman, DeCoste, McMahon, Rounsaville, & Mayes, 2011; U.S. Department of Health and Human Services, 1999) and have notable mental health problems (Barth, Gibbons, & Guo, 2006). In addition to high rates of co-occurring mental health disorders, such as depression, substance depndent parents report higher levels of parental stress (Pilowsky, Burchett, Blazer, & Ling, 2011; Reinherz, Giaconia, Hauf, Wasserman, & Paradis 2000; Testa & Smith, 2009; Weissman et al., 2006). Maternal depression has a negative impact on the development of the early parent-child relationship and the parent's ability to manage the infant's daily routines and monitor their safety (Osofsy & Lederman, 2004; Knitzer, 2007).

Substance dependent mothers tend to lack proper parenting skills that can negatively affect their children in the first three years of life when successful attachment and bonding is so imperative for optimal long-term development (Kerwin, 2005; Suchman, DeCoste, Castiglione, Legow, & Mayes, 2008). Drug-abusing mothers may also have a difficult time understanding and responding to baby's cues because the mothers are preoccupied with internal demands of craving and seeking, and then managing the alter states created by the effects of the drugs. These altered states also interfere with empathy for others and often result in the misreading of subtle and potent cues from their child regarding the child's own internal state (Mayes & Truman, 2002); cues between infants and their parents are important because they are a baby's only means of communication. An additional complication in these families is the fact that many children born to substance abusing parents are themselves addicted to substances at birth. Infants exposed prenatally to drug and alcohol are at high risk of compromised brain development and interruption of the mother-child bond (Bruskas, 2010).

Research demonstrating the developmental benefits of touch and the consequences of misattuned, hyperarousing, or abusive touch patterns, as well as of touch deprivation, is growing (e.g., Bremmer & Fogel, 2001; Cascio, 2010; Hertenstein, Verkamp, Kerestes, & Holmes, 2006; Herenstein & Weiss, 2011). It is now thought that a pattern of nurturing touch reduces developmental "costs" (Sander, 2008) that infants incur when they must continuously adjust to insensitive handling and certain types of gentle touch have been proven to calm the infant's nervous system (Field, 2001). Attuned rhythmic touch and sensitive care giving has also been linked to neuro-developmental success in children recovering from trauma (Perry & Szalavitz, 2006).

The use of infant massage with high-risk families is designed to increase attunement and ultimately create healthy attachment between parent and child through the use of touch. Research demonstrates that interventions that teach the practice of infant massage have been used successfully to establish a better bond between parents and their babies as well as to decrease parental stress and depressive moods and improve parenting skills and knowledge of child development (e.g., Cullen, Field, Escalona, & Hartshorn, 2000; Dozier et al., 2006; Feijo et al., 2006; O'Higgins, Roberts, & Glover, 2008; Onzawa et al., 2001). However, the use of infant massage interventions with substance dependent parents in early stages of recovery has not yet been evaluated.

INTERVENTION

Fostering Mindful Attachment (FMA) is a parent-infant massage and attachment intervention targeting parents in early stages of recovery from substance use disorders and their infant children. The FMA program is designed as an integrated and holistic early-intervention treatment delivery model that combines a variety of educational, clinical, and, at times, administrative and evaluative services in a single program. To broaden its usefulness in the San Francisco, California, area where it originated, the program became qualified as a court mandated parenting education course and as a visitation site for parents separated from their young children by court order.

Administered by licensed mental health professionals with advanced training in infant mental health, each two-hour class in the 10-week program combines parenting education topics, parent-infant massage instruction and practice, group interaction and discussion, short periods of mindfulness based self-awareness processes for the parents, as well as music, song, and poetry. The parenting education curriculum, conducted in an interactive discussion model, examines the topics of self-esteem, stress regulation, anger management, security, resilience, communication, substance abuse, domestic violence, and positive discipline. Each week, a topic is explored and discussed as parents are coached about understanding and responding to their infant's communications, utilizing the vehicle of touch and massage to connect with their child.

It is in the context of the parent–infant massage instruction and practice that the clinical intervention emerges. The FMA program recognizes that much of early development unfolds in and is contingent on the relational context. Group and individual learning moments that emerge from the massage practice help parents develop sensitive parenting and self-awareness capacities. Each session supports improved attachment and attunement to the individual child and to the unique qualities and features of their developmental process. The program explores the proposition that relational stability and secure attachment are inevitably connected to regulatory stability in parent and child.

A dynamic systems model of self and co-regulation underlies many of the program elements of the FMA. A complex systems approach provides a suffiently wide conceptual platform to support the tracking of moment-to-moment intersection of the dyadic interaction of two consciousnesses, bodies and nervous sytems (Fogel, 1993; Sander, 2002). Consequently, the curriculum and the interventions support awareness and acknowledgment of the child's internal state and generate recognition and support for "baby-time." Careful parent-infant massage practice gives caregivers an opportunity to learn to track the infant's real-time, nonverbal response to qualities of touch interactions (Field, 2001; Hertenstein & Weiss, 2011) and to develop new capacities to recognize and attend to their own internal states of arousal in the present moment (Ogden, Minton, & Pain, 2006). This self-awareness and the development of improved self-regulation strategies are particularly important because many of the parents have significant trauma histories. One of the goals of the program is reducing the impact of transgenerational transmission of traumatic states and nervous system templates. Mindfulness practices of self-awareness, including tracking bodily tensions, breath awareness, and redirection of thought to the present, support recovering parents' growing capacity for reflection on self-with-other.

The FMA program's focus on parental awareness of infant's internal states, the development of skills for self-regulating of affect, the calming of their child, and the development of a capacity for sustained positive parent-child interaction allows parents in early recovery from substance dependence, who themselves have a complex family history of poor attachment and attunement, to become more available in the psychological space and time they spend with their infant children. It is hypothesized that this increased attunement and connection, over the course of the intervention, will result in decreased depression and perceived stress, as well as increased knowledge of good parenting practices, better relatedness with their infant children, and improved self-efficacy for parenting.

EVALUATION METHODS

Participants

Five 10-week FMA groups were offfered between 2009 and 2011 for families who were known to the local child welfare authorities, living in a residential substance abuse treatment facility, and being followed by a social services caseworker. While more than 30 parents initially enrolled in one of these five groups, only 22 completed the intervention. Of these 22 parents, 17 participated in both the pretest and posttest interviews for the evaluation study. The current analyses are based on the results obtained from this sample of 17 parents.

Participants were predominantly single (65%) adult (M = 33.73 years; SD = 5.87) women (88%) who were recipients of government income assistance (53%). The majority described themselves as Caucasian (53%) or African American (29%) who had obtained a high school diploma/GED (41%) or some college education (35%). More than half (65%) paid rent prior to their entry into recovery; however, 18% stated being homeless. When asked if they had ever been in foster care, 18% stated that they were former foster children.

Participants' infant children were three to four month old (M = 3.45 months; SD = 2.74) females (65%) who were born with a positive toxicology screen (60%) with diverse ethnic backgrounds (35% Caucasian, 24% African American, and 18% Latino/a). Parents reported the used of crack cocaine, marijuana, heroin, methamphetamine, methadone, speed, cigarettes, and/or alcohol while pregnant. About half (53%) of the infants were living with the parent at the beginning of the intervention, 35% were in foster care, and 12% were in kinship care. At the conclusion of the intervention over three-fourths (77%) of the infants were living with their parents, 18% were in foster care and 6% were in kinship care.

Procedures

Parents who registered to complete the FMA program were contacted by a member of the research team at the residential treatment facility in which they resided. Staff of the treatment center assisted in identifying those residents who had registered for the class and provided access to the research team. Parents who agreed to participate in the evaluation study signed an Informed Consent Form prior to being interviewed. Face-to-face semi-structured interviews were conducted with parents (n = 17 across five groups) in the week prior to the first FMA class session and immediately following their last class meeting. Results from these two interviews can therefore be compared and considered as a "One Group Pre-Test Post-Test Design."

Measures

Interviews included a semi-structured demographic and program evaluation survey and three standardized instruments: the Beck Depression Inventory (BDI), the Parenting Stress Index – Short Form (PSI/SF), and the Knowledge of Infant Development Inventory (KIDI). The survey included basic questions about the parent's and infant's demographics (e.g., age, gender, ethnicity, educational level), substance use history, social support, pregnancy and birth history, and relationship with their infant child. Intervention group participants were also asked a series of open-ended questions about their experience in the FMA program. The BDI is 21-item self report instrument for measuring the severity of depression in adults (Beck, Steer, & Brown, 1996), which has been demonstrated to have high reliability and validity (Beck, Steer, & Garbin, 1988). The PSI/SF is a 36-item, standardized rating scale with established reliability and validity that provides a total stress score as well as three subscales — Parental Stress, Parent-Child Dysfuntional Interaction and Difficult Child (Abidin, 1983). The KIDI is a 58-item, standardized rating scale, also with established reliability and validity, which is designed to assess a person's knowledge of developmental processes and infant norms (MacPhee, 1981).

RESULTS

As part of the face-to-face interviews before and after the intevention, participants were asked about their interest in infant massage and about how they feel when their baby cries. Responses by all participants to these open-ended questions were systematically reviewed and similar remarks were combined into thematic groups; data presented in Table 1 and Table 2 are actual quotes from participants' remarks that are representative of each of the thematic groups of comments.

TABLE 1
Representative Participant Responses to "What is interesting about infant massage?"

Before Intervention	*After Intervention*
• . . . have been separated from my infant for months; hoping infant massage will help to get to my baby better • Bonding with my baby • It makes the baby feel better, more relaxed. Her body won't get tense. • Learn how to massage baby's body • Learn different pressure points, areas to relax the baby • Spend time with baby. Helps them grow, feel good, relax, feel close to each other • To learn how to soothe my baby	• The advice I received about bonding with baby – good tips • Everything – the teachers, the way they teach – it's intense: it's positive • The fact that I got to bond with my baby. Learned how to have patience and the pressure of massaging • Had fun. Got to massage my baby, got to visit with her and it was not boring to attend infant massage class • Helped to communicate with my baby • How we can connect with our babies, massage them, to make them comfortable, and calm them down • I got a lot of bonding with my baby and learned to communicate better. • Like that I was able to bond with my baby – I don't think it (the bond) would have been as strong without infant massage • Loved the connection you get with your baby – the bond, it's comforting • The teachers made us explore our inner deepest childhood moments • How infant massage benefits both the parent and the baby

TABLE 2
Representative Participant Responses to "How does it make you feel when your child cries?"

Before Intervention	*After Intervention*
• Anxious • Distressed because I don't know what he wants • Handicapped because I don't know what to do. • Distressing. They just can't be held. They don't understand. Will (understand) when they are older. I understand, they don't understand. • Horrible • It depends on the situation - I don't like it when giving medicine, it's hard. It's frustrating. He (son) can't communicate what's wrong. • It makes me feel discomfort because she doesn't feel good because I don't know why she's crying • Sad, angry, depressed • Sad and worried	• It makes me feel like I need to figure out if he needs something – it's a cue that he needs something from me • Concerned and frustrated • Frustrated – don't know why she's crying • I feel compassion because I want to make her feel better. • Like I need to comfort her • Like I'm needed for something and that I can take care of it. I know it's his way of communicating. • Sad • It makes me feel like I need to find out why he is crying. • Confused because sometimes I don't know why she is crying • To hurry up and do something about it

Participants were asked to report the number of happy, confused/frustrating, and sad moments they had each day with their baby (Table 3). Before the intervention 77% of parents reported there were "too many happy moments to count" each day with their babies; after attending the intervention 88% of parent reported there were "too many happy moments to count" each

TABLE 3
Participant Reports on Moments with Babies

Questions		*Frequency Before Intervention*	*Frequency After Intervention*
How many *happy* moments do you have with your baby each day?	None	0	0
	One or Two	0	0
	A Few	0	5.9% ($n = 1$)
	Several	23.5% ($n = 4$)	5.9% ($n = 1$)
	Too Many to Count	76.5% ($n = 13$)	88.2% ($n = 15$)
How many *confused and frustrated* moments do you have with your baby each day?	None	29.4% ($n = 5$)	35.3% ($n = 6$)
	One or Two	47.1% ($n = 8$)	41.2% ($n = 7$)
	A Few	17.6% ($n = 3$)	23.5% ($n = 4$)
	Several	5.9% ($n = 1$)	0
	Too Many to Count	0	0
How many *sad* moments do you have with your baby each day?	None	52.9% ($n = 9$)	52.9% ($n = 9$)
	One or Two	35.3% ($n = 6$)	47.1% ($n = 8$)
	A Few	5.9% ($n = 1$)	0
	Several	0	0
	Too Many to Count	0	0

TABLE 4
Paired Samples t-test – BDI, PSI, and KIDI

		Pretest Scores		*Posttest Scores*			
	n	*M*	*SD*	*M*	*SD*	*t*	*p*
Beck Depression Inventory (BDI)	17	9.53	5.13	8.82	5.69	.499	.624
PSI – Parent-Child Dysfunctional Interaction	17	21.82	6.72	19.06	5.66	2.021	.060
PSI – Parental Distress	17	27.35	7.44	25.29	5.37	1.192	.251
PSI – Difficult Child	17	22.59	4.03	21.82	5.57	.598	.558
PSI – Defensive Responding	17	16.06	4.15	15.35	4.65	.582	.568
PSI – Total Stress	17	71.18	14.86	67.71	15.66	.884	.390
KIDI – Not Sure	17	.120	.08	.066	.07	3.084	.007*
KIDI – Attempt	17	.826	.20	.934	.07	−2.052	.057
KIDI – Accuracy	17	.776	.09	751	.12	.784	.444
KIDI – Total Score	17	.675	.09	.703	.13	−.818	.425

*$p < .01$.

Note. M = Mean. SD = Standard Deviation. BDI range from 0 to 63, with over 40 representing extreme depression. PSI Total Stress range from 39 to 112 with higher scores representing higher stress levels. KIDI presented as ratios of (number of items)/58 possible items.

day with their babies. After the intervention parents reported a small decrease in the number of confused/frustrating moments they had with there babies each day. There was no notable change in the number of sad moments before and after the intervention.

Results from the standardized measures of parent depression, parenting stress, and knowledge of infant development are presented in Table 4. Parent depression scores were essentially the same before and after completion of the 10-week FMA program (Mean BDI total score before = 9.53 and Mean BDI total score after = 8.82). Though not statistically significant, participants reported lower parenting stress after completion of the intervention (Mean PSI total score before = 71.18; Mean PSI total score after = 67.71). All four sub-scales on the PSI also revealed trends in the direction of decreased parental stress; in particular the Parent-Child Dysfunctional Interaction scale ($p = .060$). Differences before and after the intervention in knowledge of infant development were not statistically significant, although trends demonstrated slightly higher levels of knowledge after the completion of the intervention (mean 68% items correct on pretest, mean 70% correct on posttest). Results revealed a significant decrease in the number of items on the KIDI to which participants responded "not sure" (mean 12% at pretest, mean 5% at posttest), but overall accuracy did not increase.

Participants were asked about what they learned from completing the FMA program. Responses by all participants to this open-ended question were systematically reviewed and similar remarks were combined into thematic groups; data presented in Table 5 are actual quotes from participants' responses that are representative of each of the thematic groups of comments.

DISCUSSION

Interviews were conducted with groups of parents before and after they completed a 10-week infant massage attachment intervention. Overall, parents were from a mix of different ethnicities and both genders, high-school educated, and drawing income from a government-based financial assistance program. Most of the mothers used a variety of substances while pregnant and most of the babies were born with a positive toxicology screen. Parents were motivated to participate in the infant massage program in order to bond better with their baby, to help their baby feel good, and to learn how to soothe their baby.

Parents reported a range of confused/frustrating moments each day with their babies and indicated a range of number of times they reconnected with their babies following a confusing or distressing time. Before completing the intervention, these parents, each likely ineffectively

TABLE 5
Representative Participant Responses to "What have you learned in this class about caring for your baby?"

Responses
• It helped me understand what my baby is communicating.
• I learned that there are ways to massage the baby to help in calming them.
• It taught me the importance of taking time out to stay connected.
• Learned a lot about myself and how to interact with my baby and the benefit of massage for them.
• The need to attend to her needs, read cues, and increase communication.
• Being attentive with them and interacting with them more.
• It helped in soothing baby when baby is not feeling well.
• How to love and be patient.
• How to pay attention.
• How to become more verbal with baby.

and inappropriately parented in their own childhood and therefore ill-equipped to provide a healthy and secure base for their infant, reported that when their baby cried they felt "horrible," "frustrated," "sad, angry, depressed," and "stressed, confused." In contrast, after completing the course, these parents reported that when their baby cried, although they felt frustrated, they knew their baby was "crying for need" and it was their baby's "way of communicating." Parents indicated that they learned more about infant development, about how to understand and soothe their baby, and about how to communicate with their baby. More of the infants were living with their parent at the end of the intervention than had been living with their parent at the start of the intervention.

Despite a small sample size, results from standardized measures, with the exception of the depression screening tool, are all in the expected direction — nonsignificant trends toward higher knowledge of infant development and lower parenting stress across all subscales and the overall score after completing the intervention program. Though the depression screening score was essentially unchanged after the intervention, participants reported at posttest that they more often perceived their children as less difficult. Thus, it may be that although positive changes occured in interactions between parents and infants, the consequent improvement in mood may require more time to occur. The finding that parents were less frequently "not sure" about parenting practices suggests they may have felt higher self-esteem following the intervention, though self-esteem was not measured.

Current results are based on a very small sample and should be regarded with caution. Despite this limited power to detect differences between pretest and posttest responses, notable changes emerged in participants' perceptions of their babies as "difficult." Trends in the data suggest that this intervention, when directed at parents in early recovery from substance dependence who are interested in learning infant massage, makes a difference in knowledge of infant development, parenting stress, parents' ability to read their babies' cues, to soothe their babies appropriately, and to regulate their response to their babies. That a once-per-week two-hour intervention lasting less than three months made even a perceptible impact on these psychologically damaged, substance dependent, poorly nurtured parents in their ability to connect with and understand their infant children is remarkable. Such changes might even suggest that substance dependent parents in early recovery who receive attachment interventions may be better equipped to form healthy relationships with their infant children, to parent more effectively, and to break the intergenerational cycle of child abuse and neglect. It is also possible that parents who feel better about their parenting abilities and who feel more connected to their infant children will be less likely to relapse and return to substance using behaviors, thereby further reducing rates of child maltreatment across generations.

REFERENCES

Abidin, R. R. (1983). *Parenting Stress Index manual.* Charlottesville VA: Pediatric Psychology Press.

Appleyard, K., Berlin, L. J., Rosanbalm, K. D. & Dodge, K. A. (2011). Preventing early child maltreatment: Implications from a longitudinal study of maternal abuse history, substance use problems, and offspring victimization. *Prevention Science*, *12*, 139–149.

Back, S. U. (2010). Toward an improved model of treating co-occurring PTSD and substance use disorders. *The American Journal of Psychiatry*, *167*, 11–13.

Bakermans-Kranenburg, M., Van Ijzendoorn, M., & Juffer, F. (2005). Disorganized infant attachment and preventive interventions: A review and meta-analysis. *Infant Mental Health Journal*, *26*, 191–216.

Barth, R. P., Gibbons, C., & Guo, S. (2006). Substance abuse treatment and the recurrence of maltreatment among caregivers with children living at home: A propensity score analysis. *Journal of Substance Abuse Treatment, 30*, 93–104.

Beck, A. T., Steer, R. A., & Brown, G. K. (1996). *Manual for Beck Depression Inventory-II*. San Antonio, TX: Psychological Corporation.

Beck, A. T., Steer, R. A., & Garbin, M. G. (1988). Psychometric properties of the Beck Depression Inventory: Twenty-five years of evaluation. *Clinical Psychology Review, 8*, 77–100.

Berglund, M., Thelander, S., Salaspuro, M., Franck, J., Andreasson, S., & Ojehagen, A. (2003). Treatment of alcohol abuse: An evidence-based review. *Alcoholism: Clinical & Experimental Research, 27*, 1645–1656.

Bowlby, J. (1969). *Attachment and loss: Vol. 1. Attachment*. New York, NY: Basic Books.

Bremmer, G., & Fogel, A. (2004). The salience of touch and physical contact during infancy: Unraveling some of the mysteries of the somesthetic sense. In *Blackwell Handbook of Infant Development* (chap. 13). Hoboken, NJ: Blackwell Publishing.

Briggs, E. C., Thompson, R., Ostrowski, S., & Lekwauwa, R. (2011). Psychological, health, behavioral, and economic impact of child maltreatment. In *Violence against women and children, Volume 1. Mapping the terrain*. (pp. 77–97). Washington, DC: American Psychological Association.

Bruskas, D. (2008). Children in foster care: A vulnerable population at risk. *Journal of Child and Adolescent Psychiatric Nursing, 21*, 70–77.

Cascio, C. J. (2010). Somatosensory processing in neurodevelopmental disorders. *Journal of Neurodevelopmental Disorders, 2*, 62–69.

Compton, W. M., Conway, K. P., Stinson, F. S., & Grant, B. F. (2006). Changes in the prevalence of major depression and comorbid substance use disorders in the United States between 1991–1992 and 2001–2002. *The American Journal of Psychiatry, 163*, 2141–2147.

Cullen, C., Field, T., Escalona, A., & Hartshorn, K. (2000). Father-infant interactions are enhanced by massage therapy. *Early Child Development and Care, 164*, 41–47.

Dixon, L., Browne, K., & Hamilton-Giachritsis, C. (2009). Patterns of risk and protective factors in the intergenerational cycle of maltreatment. *Journal of Family Violence, 24*, 111–122.

Dore, M. M., & Doris, J. M. (1998). Preventing child placement in substance-abusing families: Research-informed practice. *Child Welfare: Journal of Policy, Practice, and Program, 77*, 407–426.

Dozier, M., Peloso, E., Lindhiem, O., Gordon, M. K., Manni, M., Sepulveda, S., & Levine, S. (2006). Developing evidence-based interventions for foster children: An example of a randomized clinical trial with infants and toddlers. *Journal of Social Issues, 62*, 767–785.

Fang, X. & Corso, P. S. (2007). Child maltreatment, youth violence, and intimate partner violence: Developmental relationships. *American Journal of Preventive Medicine, 33*, 281–290.

Feijo, L., Hernandez-Reif, M., Field, T., Burns, W., Valley-Gray, S., & Simco, E. (2006). Mothers' depressed mood and anxiety levels are reduced after massaging their preterm infants. *Infant Behavior & Development, 29*, 476–480.

Field, T. (2001). *Touch*. Cambridge, MA: MIT Press.

Fogel, A. (1993). *Developing through relationships: Origins of communication, self and culture*. Chicago, IL: University of Chicago Press.

Fraiberg, S., Adelson, E., & Shapiro, V. (1975). Ghosts in the nursery: A psychoanalytic approach to the problems of impaired infant-mother relationships. *Journal of the American Academy of Child Psychiatry, 14*, 387–421.

Frederico, M. M., Jackson, A. L., & Black, C. M. (2008). Understanding the impact of abuse and neglect on children and young people referred to a therapeutic program. *Journal of Family Studies, 14*, 342–361.

Hertenstein, M., Verkamp, J., Kerestes, A., & Holmes, R. (2006). The communicative functions of touch in humans, non human primates, and rats: A review and synthesis of the empirical research. *Genetic, Social, and General Psychology Monographs, 132*, 5–94.

Hertenstein, M. J., & Weiss, S. J. (Eds.). (2011). *The handbook of touch: Neuroscience, behavioral, and applied perspectives*. New York, NY: Springer Publications.

Kerwin, M. E. (2005). Collaboration between child welfare and substance abuse fields: Combined treatment programs for mothers. *Journal of Pediatric Psychology, 30*, 581–597.

Knitzer, J. (2007). Putting knowledge into policy: Toward an infant-toddler policy agenda. *Infant Mental Health Journal, 28*, 237–245.

Lansford, J. E., Dodge, K. A., Pettit, G. S., & Bates, J. E. (2010). Does physical abuse in early childhood predict substance use in adolescence and early adulthood? *Child Maltreatment, 15*, 190–194.

MacPhee, D. (1981). Manual for the knowledge of infant development inventory. Unpublished manuscript, University of North Carolina.

Mayes, L., & Truman, S. (2002). Substance abuse and parenting. In *Handbook of parenting: Vol. 4: Social conditions and applied parenting* (2nd ed., pp. 329–359). Mahwah, NJ: Lawrence Erlbaum Associates.

McLellan, A., Lewis, D. C., O'Brien, C. P., Kleber, H. D. (2000). Drug dependence, a chronic medical illness: Implications for treatment, insurance, and outcomes evaluation. *The Journal of the American Medical Association, 284*, 1689–1695.

Nadel, J., & Tremblay-Leveau, H. (1999). Early perception of social contingencies and interpersonal timing: Dyadic and triadic paradigms. In P. Rochat (Ed.), *Early social cognition* (pp. 189–212). Hillsdale, NJ: Lawrence Erlbaum Associates.

Ogden, P., Minton, K., & Pain, C. (2006). *Trauma and the body: A sensorimotor approach to psychotherapy*. New York, NY: Norton.

O'Higgins, M., Roberts, I., & Glover, V. (2008). Postnatal depression and mother and infant outcomes after infant massage. *Journal of Affective Disorders, 109*, 189–192.

Onzawa, K., Glover, V., Adams, D., Modi, N., & Kumar, R. (2001). Infant massage improves mother-infant interaction for mothers with postnatal depression. *Journal of Affective Disorders, 63*, 201–207.

Osofsky, J. D., & Lederman, C. (2004). Healing the child in juvenile court. In J. D. Osofsky (Ed.), *Young children and trauma: Intervention and treatment* (pp. 221–241). New York: Guilford Press.

Paolucci, E. O., Genuis, M. L. & Violato, C. (2001). A meta-analysis of the published research on the effects of child sexual abuse. *Journal of Psychology: Interdisciplinary and Applied, 135*, 17–36.

Perry, B., & Szalavitz, M. (2006). *The boy who was raised as a dog and other stories from a child psychiatrist's notebook: What traumatized children can teach us about loss, love, and healing*. New York, NY: Basic Books.

Pilowshy, D. J., Burchett, B., Blazer, D. G., & Ling, W. (2011). Depressive symptoms, substance use, and HIV-related high-risk behaviors among opioid-dependent individuals: Results from the Clinical Trials Network. *Substance Use & Misuse, 46*, 1716–1725.

Redelinghuys, J., & Dar, K. (2008). A survey of parents receiving treatment for substance dependence: The impact on their children. *Journal of Substance Use, 13*, 37–48.

Reinherz, H. Z., Giaconia, R. M., Hauf, A. M. C., Wasserman, M. S., & Paradis, A. D. (2000). General and specific childhood risk factors for depression and drug disorders by early adulthood. *Journal of the American Academy of Child & Adolescent Psychiatry, 39*, 223–231.

Sander, L. (2002). Thinking differently; Principles of process in living systems and the specificity of being known. *Psychoanalytic Dialogues, 12*, 11–42.

Sander, L. (2008). *Living systems, evolving consciousness, and the emerging person: A selection of papers from the life work of Louis Sander*. New York, NY: The Analytic Press/Taylor & Francis Group.

Schore, A. (1994). *Affect regulation and the origin of the self: Neurobiology of emotional development*. Hillsdale, NJ: Lawrence Erlbaum Associates.

Schwerdtfeger, K., & Nelson Goff, B. (2007). Intergenerational transmission of trauma: Exploring mother-infant prenatal attachment. *Journal of Traumatic Stress, 20*, 39–51.

Silver, J., & Dicker, S. (2007). Mental health assessment of infants in foster care. *Child Welfare League of America, 88*(2), 35–55.

Suchman, N. E., DeCoste, C., McMahon, T. J., Rounsaville, B. , & Mayes, L. (2011). The mothers and toddlers program, an attachment-based parenting intervention for substance-using women: Results at 6-week follow-up in a randomized clinical pilot. *Infant Mental Health Journal, 32*, 427–449.

Suchman, N., DeCoste, C., Castiglioni, N., Legow, N., & Mayes, L. (2008). The mothers and toddlers program. Preliminary findings from an attachment-based parenting intervention for substance abusing mothers. *Psychoanalytic Psychology, 25*, 499–517.

Testa, M. F., & Smith, B. (2009). Prevention and drug treatment. *The Future of Children, 19*, 147–168.

U.S. Department of Health and Human Services. (1999). *Blending perspectives and building common ground: A report to Congress on substance abuse and child protection*. Washington, DC: U.S. Government Printing Office.

Walsh, W. A., Dawson, J., Mattingly, M. J. (2010). How are we measuring resilience following child maltreatment? Is the research adequate and consistent? What is the impact on research, practice, and policy? *Trauma, Violence, and Abuse, 11*, 27–41.

Weissman, M. M., Wickramaratne, P., Nomura, Y., Warner, V., Pilowsky, D., & Verdeli, H. (2006). Offspring of depressed parent: 20 years later. *The American Journal of Psychiatry, 163*, 1001–1008.

Zielinski, D. S. (2009). Child maltreatment and adult socioeconomic well-being. *Child Abuse and Neglect, 33*, 666–678.

Fostering Relationships with Children Who are "Too Much to Handle"

Saralyn Ruff
Julia Baron

Parenting yields unique challenges for adolescent-aged foster youth. Given their age, past trauma, lack of social support, and lack of resources, foster youth are at increased risk for mental health problems, substance abuse, and homelessness compared with nonfoster youth. Many pregnant and parenting adolescent-aged foster youth are at high risk for perpetuating the same dynamics that they themselves experienced, specifically of having their children placed in foster care. This intergenerational trauma cycle will likely continue without interventions focused on the psychological, emotional, developmental, and social experiences of both parents and children. Moreover, interventions must also focus on those implementing the interventions and working with these youth. Staff working with foster youth have high burnout and turnover rates, resulting in inconsistent service provision and disrupted relationships for the youth. Fostering Relationships is a free, theory-based resource that works toward addressing the aforementioned challenges by promoting the development of healthy relationships between foster youth and staff, and between foster youth and their children. This paper uses a case example, a review of the literature, and discussion of underlying theory to detail the need for relationship-focused intervention and the benefits of fostering relationships in supporting staff and pregnant and parenting foster youth.

When she was 10 years old, Donna's mother placed her in foster care because "she was too much to handle." Her mother, Susan, had recently given birth to another child and felt overwhelmed by trying to care for both an adolescent and an infant. Donna, like many children in the foster care system, was ordered to participate in mental health services. Donna had been referred numerous times before but had never stayed in treatment longer than a few months. The system's solution was to not only continue the referrals but also to increase their number. The concern was that Donna was traumatized and needed someone to help process her past and present life events and choices. The unexamined variable, however, was the role of the system in perpetuating this trauma by increasing the number and not quality of relationships in Donna's life.

Even in her mother's care, Donna was all too familiar with the foster care system. Her mother, Susan, was a teenage foster child when Donna was born, and so Donna was born into the foster care system. While living with her mother, multiple reports were made to Child Protective Services (CPS), alleging that Susan had physically abused Donna. One report indicated that Susan had hit Donna in the face with a belt. None of the claims was substantiated, and Donna never confirmed or denied being abused. Susan did share that she used corporal punishment to handle Donna's acting out and episodes of anger. Donna retained a scar on her forehead that she refuses, even 10 years later, to talk about.

Donna's first foster parents provided great structure and consistency, and Donna became less aggressive and had fewer outbursts. The foster family had two biological children whom they treated differently from Donna. Donna explained that the biological family often ate dinner together while Donna was sent to her room to eat. The family made it clear that they were not interested in participating in any school meetings. Clearly, the family was willing to provide a safe home but not a family.

Donna learned to be self-reliant and independent. At school, she had few friends and often ate lunch alone. She appeared to be much more comfortable alone than with others. After a brief relationship in her senior year of high school, Donna found out that she was pregnant. She was unsure of the father's interest and commitment to the child. Furthermore, she was unsure of how to raise this child and what support she would receive. This scared her, but she was committed to having her baby.

The caseworker assigned to Donna's case was Jill, a 21-year-old counselor at a community-based treatment facility. This was Jill's first job after graduating from a prestigious nearby university. She had been a psychology major and planned to return to graduate school to study social work. Jill was both excited and scared about her new job, often feeling unprepared and ill-equipped, but she wanted to gain experience to make her a stronger graduate school applicant and student. Jill had a strong mind and a big heart but minimal experience or training.

Jill was given Donna's impressively large file, containing many papers but little information. She was asked to meet with Donna, build a relationship, and provide her assistance in preparing for her unborn child — three seemingly simple tasks for a 21-year-old novice. However, these three tasks would require time, skill, resources, and luck and as she would soon learn, would be near impossible. Donna met Jill in a local coffee shop for their first meeting, introduced herself, sat down, and said nothing for the remainder of their time. The second and third meetings were the same. In their fourth meeting, Donna yelled at Jill and threw a pen across the room at her after Jill asked her how her week was. Jill was mortified, as a community-based counselor, having others witness her failures to connect with Donna. She dreaded future sessions and carried anxiety to each meeting, transparent to anyone passing by, especially Donna. Jill began to interpret Donna's behaviors to mean that Donna was clearly apathetic about forming a relationship. She requested that her supervisor close the case until Donna was invested in, and ready for, treatment. What Jill did not realize, however, was that Donna's behaviors were cries for help. Donna was testing Jill, trying to see if she could begin to trust her, trying to see if and how Jill would deal with seeing the "bad" sides of Donna. Donna was trying to cut to the chase and to learn if she could rely on Jill for the help and support she so desperately craved.

Unfortunately, the cases of Donna and of Jill are all too common. Without much thought, foster youth are asked every day to trust people, even after years of experiences that have taught them that people are not to be trusted. When they show caution, they are categorized as resistant and defiant. Simultaneously, staff working with these youth show up to work every day with hope and good intentions. They look for resources, supervision, and training to guide their work. They care about their clients and are willing to do whatever it takes to help. However, they soon learn that there are no answers, limited resources, and endless work, resulting in vicarious trauma, burnout, and turnover. The combination of high burnout and turnover in a population that works with clients deserving longevity and consistency results in a system that consistently does the opposite of what these youth need and, worse yet, confirms the message foster youth have heard too many times; that is, adults give up, especially on them, because they are "too much to handle."

In this paper, we review many of the complex dynamics unique to teen parents and specifically, unique to pregnant and parenting foster youth like Donna. We discuss key theoretical tenets of attachment theory and the Bridges' Transition Framework, useful in understanding and assisting pregnant and parenting foster youth, their children, and the parent-child relationship. We also discuss the lack of resources for staff working with pregnant and parenting foster youth as well as the resulting staff burnout and turnover. Lastly, we will introduce Fostering Relationships, a curriculum available to guide staff's work with pregnant and parenting foster youth. In particular, we provide a description of this theory- and research-oriented curriculum, focused on its potential to support both the staff working with teen-headed households and the teens themselves.

PREGNANT AND PARENTING YOUTH

Some purport that the negative impacts of adolescent-headed families are overstated; specifically, they suggest that teen parents show evidence of increased maturity, improved decision making, greater independence, and decreased risk taking behavior (Clemmens, 2003; Herrman, 2006, 2007). Although this may be true in some circumstances, there is general agreement that, even under ideal conditions, teen parenting yields unique challenges. Moreover, these challenges are far reaching, affecting the child, parent, and parent-child relationship (Herrman, 2006).

Children of teen parents face unique challenges and often increased risks. For example, teen parents are less likely to seek out early prenatal care; consequently, their children are more likely to be hospitalized and to have chronic health problems (Hoffman, 2006). Also, down the road, children of teen parents are more likely to be homeless, incarcerated, and to drop out of high school (Healthy Teen Network, 2007). Overall, the challenges that teen parents and their infants face early in life are likely to have lifelong implications.

Many of the teen parents themselves experience multiple challenges including, but not limited to, a loss of personal freedom, participation in age-appropriate rituals and events, social isolation, and economic hardship. For example, teen parents are less likely to graduate from high school or to obtain a secondary degree (Herrman, 2010; Hoffman & Maynard, 2008). As a result, these young parents experience fewer employment options and decreased economic freedom. This directly influences these teens' personal well-being, resources available for parenting, and ultimately, their strategies for, as well as perceptions of, parenting.

Teen parents often see themselves as more isolated from friends and social networks, which inhibit their involvement in age-appropriate events. Many of these youth report feeling ostracized from previous social circles and excluded from developmentally appropriate occasions. These experiences can be associated with feelings of isolation and depression that influence their personal well-being, resulting in social anxiety and withdrawal. Many of these youth are at increased risk for not completing high school, not only because of the logistical challenges in balancing parenthood and school work but also because of the pain evoked by being an outsider at school. These feelings of isolation, depression, and decreased self-esteem, paired with the actualization of their consequences (e.g., high school dropout), greatly impact their ability to parent successfully.

Teen parents and their children are at increased risk for relational challenges. Many of the challenges that exist for the parent and/or children place strain on the parent-child relationship and impede the bonding process. A parent who feels socially isolated or depressed may begin to feel resentment toward the child. Or a child with chronic health problems may be more difficult to soothe, introducing additional difficulty to the parent-infant bonding process. In sum, individual challenges associated with teen parenting often have systemic impacts, sometimes to the detriment of the parent-child relationship. We elaborate in a discussion of attachment theory, below.

In examining the increased risk of teen parenting, it is important to note that the relationship between teen parenting and increased strain on the parent, child, and parent-child bond are not causative. That is, being a teen parent does not necessarily cause increased risk. Rather, many extraneous factors increase the risk for both teen pregnancy and at-risk development (i.e., poverty, lack of resources, intergenerational patterns). Thus, systemic interventions, focused on addressing the complexity of and intersection between these factors, are required to support positive child development.

Pregnant and Parenting Foster Parents

Since 2005, the incidence of teen pregnancy has increased annually. Between 15 and 20 percent of women have a teen pregnancy in the United States (Savio Beers & Hollo, 2009). For foster youth, teen pregnancy is even more common; young women in foster care are 2.5 times more likely to become pregnant by age 19 compared with teens not in foster care (Chapin Hall, 2006). Half of young women who have been in the foster care system have been pregnant at least once before age 19; one quarter of these women have been pregnant multiple times (Chapin Hall, 2006). Clearly, foster youth are at high risk for teen pregnancy. Pregnant and parenting foster youth are also less likely to have resources and support to assist with the challenges associated with teen parenting (Chapin Hall, 2006). Consequently, teen-headed households and pregnant and parenting foster youth in particular require support services grounded in theory and research that promote healthy parent-child relationship development.

Given their past traumatic experiences and lack of social support, teen foster youth are often underprepared and ill-equipped to raise their infants and young children. These youth are at greater risk for mental health problems, substance abuse, and homelessness compared with nonfoster youth. One-fifth of all foster youth become homeless as adults, and one-fourth are incarcerated within two years of leaving the system (O'Hare, 2001). Compared with nonfoster youth, when these youth become parents, their access to resources and support generally decreases. To clarify, many nonfoster teen parents continue to live with their families, resulting in multigenerational family structures to offer support and assistance to the teen parent and infant (Savio et al., 2009). However, foster youth often do not have this support. Rather, foster youth often run away from their placements once they learn that they are pregnant, resulting in increased disruption in support services and an exacerbation of the strain and risk placed on these families (Dworsky & DeCoursey, 2009).

In sum, the teen's age, lack of resources, and history of trauma places the youth at high risk for perpetuating the same dynamics that he/she experienced. As a result, many of the children of pregnant and parenting foster youth also end up in the foster care system. This intergenerational trauma cycle will likely continue without interventions that focus on the psychological, emotional, developmental, social, and educational experiences of both parents and children. This cycle is demonstrated in the case of Donna.

CURRENT RESOURCES

There are many questions and challenges with respect to working with youth like Donna, especially for the front-line staff who are most likely to work with these youth but who often have little training. However, many of the programs designed to assist pregnant and parenting foster youth focus on parenting education and case management, not on relationships. As a result, staff members do not focus on the bonding and attachment between the parent and child. Or, when they do, they are often left to rely on anecdotal and experiential techniques that, despite their potential success, limit generalization to larger samples of teen parents and foster youth. Worse yet, many of these anecdotal techniques are nonoptimal or ineffective, failing to adequately assess and/or address the needs of these adolescent-headed families. It is time to expand on extant resources, centered on prevention and case management, to focus on strategies that support healthy relationships within families like Donna and her baby.

When developing appropriate resources, interventionists must be mindful of barriers to care when working with foster youth. One common barrier is a youth's resistance to services. This may be due to a myriad of factors including, but not limited to, their own negative experiences with past service providers, their fears of being deemed a "bad" parent or being reported to the system, their lack of resources and support in obtaining and utilizing resources, and their developmentally appropriate struggles with balancing dependence and independence. As we can imagine, these are all likely fears for Donna. Interventions must be mindful of these complexities and how they influence rapport building and retention rates. Moreover, interventionists must be prepared for these normative challenges so as not to take them personally and react by leaving or getting angry, thereby perpetuating the youth's beliefs that adults leave, and that they do not belong in lasting, healthy relationships.

A second barrier to service provision for pregnant and parenting foster youth involves the staff working to address their mental health needs. Specifically, professionals working with this population are often overworked, underpaid, and underprepared. Out of nearly 20 percent of graduates from accredited Marriage and Family Therapy Master's programs in the United States who work with foster care clinical issues, fewer than 5 percent of these professionals received graduate coursework on adoption, foster care, or child development (Weir, Fife, Whiting, & Blazewick, 2008). Furthermore, because many of these staff have not received adequate preparation to work with this challenging population and because the current economic climate does not support the ongoing training and support these staff deserve, many struggle with vicarious trauma and burnout. Consequently, there is high turnover in this field to the detriment of these youth who deserve consistent and skilled care. Many staff working with these youth burn out and leave, or remain physically present but psychically absent. Between 20 and 40 percent of foster care caseworkers leave their jobs each year (Nittoli, 2003). This turnover exacerbates the relational stressors many of these teen parents experience; the loss, or lack of availability, of staff due to burnout impairs client-provider relationships and decreases the efficacy of interventions. Consequently, this population needs support and resources to guide optimal service provision by enhancing staff members' sense of support, efficacy, and job satisfaction.

UNDERLYING THEORY

To shift to a focus on relationships, we need to work on empowering clients to develop positive relationships with themselves and their children rather than simply focusing on the case management of foster youth and their children. To achieve this we need to focus on developing lasting relationships between clients and staff. This requires that we offer staff the resources and training they both desire and deserve. Two frameworks that have great impact and relevance in foster care and that guide the planned Fostering Relationships program are attachment theory and the Bridges' Transition Framework.

Attachment Theory

Attachment theory is an ethological theory focused on an individual's development (Bowlby, 1982). Specifically, attachment theory focuses on the development and maintenance of attachment bonds, originating in early life between infants and primary caregivers, motivated by a desire to maintain proximity with a caregiver and promote individual survival. Attachment theory focuses on the biological bases of attachment and the critical influence of attachment bonds on one's personality development, adjustment, and subsequent relationships over the life course (Cassidy, 2008).

The quality of interactions between a primary caregiver and infant shapes the attachment bond (Bowlby, 1988). In particular, repeated interactions in infancy shape the expectations and beliefs children construct about others through the development of internal working models (Bowlby, 1973). Internal working models are mental representations based on the development of cognitions that contribute to the endogenous regulation of the attachment system. These representational systems act as interpretive filters that help to organize individual experience in accordance with expectations.

According to attachment theory, parents who are able to adequately understand their infants' internal states and respond sensitively help to regulate their physiological states. A mother who feeds her hungry baby and uses loving words to convey that she understands him and reassures him lends her baby some of her strength. She provides her son with the food he needs, but also helps him to calm down so that he can eat and have a good experience while connecting with his mother. This attunement helps the child build the capacity to manage states of arousal. Further, her assurance helps the infant have a balanced internal experience, preventing him from being either overstimulated or understimulated. This balance supports the child to be able to remain organized and to facilitate the ability to explore and learn.

Early relationships and experiences influence the child throughout his lifespan. To return to our previous example, fast forwarding five or six years, this child will have developed some ability to notice, label, and think about his feelings of crankiness or tiredness and link it to the self-observation that he is hungry. He then will feel comfortable asking an adult for something to eat, knowing that he can trust adults to provide nurturance. This ability to organize his experience, think about its implications, and take action to meet his needs is developed over time and in the context of an attuned, responsive relationship.

Many foster children experience patterned disruptions in their primary relationships early in life that shape their perceptions of others and, consequently, of their social interactions and relationships (Bretherton & Munholland, 2008; Bowlby, 1973). Many of these children experience extremely difficult childhoods, including abuse and/or neglectful parenting, removal from the caregiver, placement in one or more foster homes, and so on. Through the development of cognition, foster children translate these early experiences into internal working models, or beliefs of the world, that adults are temporary, not reliable, or worse yet, are abusive and neglectful. These experiences also translate into internal working models about the self. A foster child may begin to rationalize that disruptions experienced in early relationships were a response to personal worth. That is, a child may begin to internalize the external conflict that has disrupted his world and begin to believe that he deserved or caused the conflict.

As a result of their early experiences, many foster youth learn to become fiercely independent or distrustful of others from an early age as a defense against being hurt again. Others grow up without a sense of family and belonging, and thus, long to create families of their own. These desires and independence, however, are often not developmentally appropriate; simply, these youth are not ready to handle the responsibilities associated with the adult roles they often assume from a young age (i.e., parenthood). Moreover, negative internal working models pervade a sense of self and consequently influence their relationships, particularly with their children. These relationships are at risk for self-perpetuation, resulting in intergenerational patterns of disrupted attachment. And, without the tools or know how, many of these youth are at high risk of repeating the only type of parenting they know.

With respect to Donna, an understanding of attachment theory clearly offers direction for Jill. To clarify, although the specifics of Donna's relationship with her mother during the early years of her life are unknown, it is clear that there were challenges that influenced the attachment process. Donna's mother, Susan, was herself a teen mother and, as a result, most likely experienced great challenges in caring for her daughter. Susan had limited resources and family support. Moreover, the circumstances of her own foster care placement were a result of a lack of positive parenting and loving early relationships. Thus, in many ways, Donna was perpetuating an intergenerational cycle of foster care placement, teen pregnancy, and unstable relationships.

As noted, the actual experiences of Donna's upbringing were unknown. Allegations of abuse were made but not substantiated. It was clear, however, that the relational experiences that Donna had from an early age impaired her sense of self and others. Donna learned early on not to confirm or deny the challenges of her relationship with her mother. Her lack of response either way indicated an absence of trust and openness in her relationships. It also reflected the common experience of many abused children; that is, Donna loved and feared her mom. Because of this, Donna would not disclose their past and would remain in an unhealthy relationship.

Through the repeated experiences of unsubstantiated abuse, Donna also learned that the child welfare system was unable to intervene to help Susan and Donna. This confirmed Donna's experience that adults felt, in general, unsure of how to help her. Susan was the one to make the final decision to place Donna in foster care. Susan communicated that she did not feel able to handle Donna's behaviors — that she was simply "too much" — a message that clearly impaired parent-child bonding. Moreover, Susan decided to give Donna up at the same time Susan she was having a second child. This left Donna with an understanding that she was not worth a mother's continued efforts and that she was replaceable. This message would have clear impacts on Donna's internal working model and was at the core of Donna's treatment and her reluctance to enter into a therapeutic relationship.

Donna's move into foster care resulted in changes in Donna's behavior that were perceived by outsiders to be positive. She quickly adapted to a new home, without much processing of the great change that had occurred in her life. Some noted increased compliance with rules and authority and decreased depression and anxiety. However, others saw this as a defeat: Donna had simply learned to accept that she did not belong in a loving family and resigned to an independent existence of living alone on the downstairs level while the "family" resided upstairs. Donna remained isolated at school and without relationships. Again, this reinforced Donna's reluctance to build and utilize new relationships in her life, including a relationship with Jill.

The Bridges' Transition Framework

The Bridges' Transition Framework is an evidence-based framework focused on teaching foster youth about the process of transition (Van Ryzin, Mills, Kelban, Vars, & Chamberlain, 2011). This framework was initially used in workplace settings as a means to understand the impact that change has on employees. This framework has since been expanded and applied to many populations, including foster youth. Use of the Bridges' Transition Framework has shown to increase youth's openness, which is associated with a decrease in internalizing symptoms (Van Ryzin et al., 2011). In particular, this framework assists individuals to distinguish between changes and transitions. A change, the external event that a person encounters, is discrete, with a clear beginning and end (e.g., getting a new job, leaving foster care, giving birth). A transition, on the other hand, is a person's internal reaction to the change, his subjective experience that the new event has instigated. Transitions also connote a process that occurs over time. That is, people undergo a process of internal transformation in order to adjust to their new external situation. Transitions deal with the psychological and can often entail a complicated mix of feelings and thoughts.

Ideally, when a change occurs, especially a major one, a person can move through transitions in a full and open way. This means that in healthy transitions, people come to accept and deal with their feelings around a change and integrate a new understanding of themselves and the world. While it does not necessarily mean that a person is happy with the change, he/she has been able to put it into perspective and can deal with it as effectively as possible. Clearly, some experiences are more challenging than others and require greater amounts of time and help. A transition does not go as well if the process is short-circuited. For example, imagine what happens when a person is confronted with a particular ending but ignores or minimizes the feelings of loss that are associated with that ending. The result is that aspects of the emotional impact fail to be integrated and the person cannot have a full and realistic acceptance of an experience. In other words, one might say that it is a loss that has been so intensely defended against that at some level the person may feel as if it never really occurred. Another result could be that he/she becomes less able to face minor losses in daily life, as they are reminders of the earlier, more significant loss.

As we know, foster youth experience great instability and inconsistency throughout their childhood. In their homes of origin, these children are likely to have experienced abuse and neglect, followed by removal, causing great upheavals and changes in their world. These changes continue to occur once in the foster care system. Half of all foster youth change schools four or more times

(Courtney, Piliavin, Grogan-Kaylor, & Nesmith, 2001); one-third of these children experience eight or more foster home placements (Pecora et al., 2005). Too often, foster youth are taught to pack their bags quickly and move on with little assistance, or encouragement, to process the transition. Consequently, many of these children are never really taught healthy ways to process or understand change and transition. As pregnant and parenting teens, many foster youth are not equipped to process and prepare for the transition to parenthood or to guide their children through transitions of their own.

Pregnant and parenting foster youth are at a crossroads of a number of different transitions, including the move to independent living, late teen and early adult identity formation, and the acquisition of greater capacity as a parent. Furthermore, many foster youth become pregnant during difficult times in their lives (Dworsky & DeCoursey, 2009). Donna became pregnant at a key transition point in her life, at the time she moved out of her foster home and became independent. This was driven by a desire to start a family, but her past experiences and lack of resources complicated the already challenging task of parenting. Many call the transition out of foster care the transition to independence; however, Donna had made that transition many years before. The transition she was making, instead, like many other foster youth, was one to starting her own family. It is at this time that Donna began to show signs of hope in her desire to keep her child. She did not know the father well and was unsure of his commitment to the relationship or child. This was almost irrelevant to Donna. What was important was that she had the hope that she could create a family. Albeit scary and against the odds, this was the first glimpse shown in many years that she believed she deserved, and was capable of having, a loving relationship.

To learn to process transitions, the Bridges' Transition Framework offers three phases: "Endings," "the Neutral Zone," and "New Beginnings." Each change ushers in an Ending. In this phase, a person grapples with the ending of something that was known. For Donna, her childhood is ending. After never getting the childhood she may have desired, she is forced to move forward and now focus on the needs of her own child. One of the significant tasks for someone such as Donna during this phase is to take accurate stock of what is changing, what is being lost, and what will remain. It is important to acknowledge the feelings associated with this process, which often include anger, anxiety, worry, and sadness.

The next phase in the Bridges' Transition Framework is the Neutral Zone, which, as the name implies, is an in-between time when the earliest shock of the change has passed, there has been a shift in perception and identification with the past, but there is nothing yet to fill the empty space. In the Bridges' Transition Framework, it is a time of chaos and creativity. The chaos arises from the feelings of confusion around what to do next and how to adapt. The creativity reflects the possibilities that arise because Endings can lead to the exploration of new paths, identifications, and ways of coping. Here, much of the work of transitions is accomplished. The feelings during this phase tend to include anxiety, confusion, and disorientation. For Donna, the feelings of confusion will be strong when it comes to becoming a mother, but there will be great room for creativity in deciding how to become the mother that she hopes she can be, rather than the mother that she had.

The final phase of the Bridges' Transition Framework is New Beginnings. At this phase, the person has arrived with a feeling of comfort at a new understanding of his situation and sense of identity. For Donna, this is when she begins to feel capable and no longer unsure of how to bond with her child. She is no longer panicked by the sound of her baby's cries; she can predict his response and feels attuned to his needs. This does not mean that she understands her child completely or that she no longer feels overwhelmed by the responsibly of parenting. Rather, it means that she has more or less faced these feelings, and has formed a perspective that allows her to function as a parent.

FOSTERING RELATIONSHIPS

Fostering Relationships is a resource that works towards addressing the aforementioned challenges. Fostering Relationships empowers the creation of relationships between foster youth and staff, and between foster youth and their children. Specifically, this program offers support to direct service providers to benefit the youth. To accommodate these professionals' needs and have the greatest reach, Fostering Relationships is a free, research- and theory-informed intervention. This resource is not intended to be a comprehensive program that can meet all of the clinical needs of foster youth, young parents, and their children. Rather, it is a time-limited, curriculum-driven program that is designed to support staff and to offer a springboard to begin the process of reflection by these young parents — on their inner experiences as teenagers or young adults — and on the internal world of their infants and children.

Format of Fostering Relationships

Available on the Internet, Fostering Relationships offers resources and support to users. Resources include a forum to connect with other staff, "ask the expert," resource recommendations, synopses of pertinent theoretical perspectives, and curricula that incorporate theory and offer a guide for staff intervention.

Fostering Relationships has value in an array of settings. The curriculum can function as a tool for therapists who are already working on these parenting issues with their clients and can also be used by program staff (e.g., case managers, group home staff, social workers) who are likely to spend the most time with this population of clients. Simply, the curriculum provides a structured way for these often overworked staff to interact with youth and assists them in remaining focused on the key mechanism of change — relationships.

Curricula available through Fostering Relationships are offered in card-based formats to promote ease of use and accessibility. Each card is structured in the same design, offering a quote, reflection, and an action. The consistency of format promotes clarity and steadiness, allowing the youth to have some sense of expectation to guide an otherwise overwhelming process. On each card, a quote offers a direction for starting a conversation. The quote allows the staff the opportunity to introduce an idea using another person's words and to step outside the "expert" role that so many youth, and new staff, resist. Moreover, the client has the opportunity to make his/her own meaning of an otherwise abstract quote, personalizing the session. Thus, the quote allows both personalization and distance — two necessary components of the push and pull often experienced in the treatment of foster youth.

The reflection on each card of the curriculum guides the conversation further by offering thought-provoking questions intended to promote a discussion of the key theoretical and relational concepts. Similar to quotations, the reflections act as a guide rather than as a directive, allowing youth to discuss the content at their comfort. Lastly, the action on each card assists the client to translate these concepts into practice, applying the ideas to practices of daily routine, thought, and interaction. These cards not only offer a framework to assist conversation but also provide for the flexibility that is necessary when working with these youth.

Underlying Theory

The goal of Fostering Relationships is to support clients to build positive relationships. In particular, the goal is to help these clients increase their ability to identify and think about their own feelings — a developmentally appropriate preoccupation of adolescence — as well as those of their children in order to support healthy attachment. To this end, the program is grounded in attachment theory and guided by the Bridges' Transition Framework.

Attachment theory is at the heart of the Fostering Relationships curriculum. This resource emphasizes the importance of relationships to our development, sense of well-being, and ability to function in the world while recognizing that being connected to others also presents ongoing challenges in many forms. Relationships can sustain our emotional needs and promote positive development, but they also require work. Fostering Relationships focuses on assisting parents to be more aware of the self (e.g., triggers, how their own childhood experiences influence them presently) and more attuned to their baby to promote healthy relationship development. Specifically, the curriculum offers structured questions that encourage conversations about the parent's past relational experiences, current reactions to experiences, and future hopes.

Fostering Relationships also serves as a resource for staff working with these youth, guiding a focus on relationships and principles of attachment. Specifically, Fostering Relationships offers the staff structure for their work to increase their sense of support and efficacy. Moreover, these resources creates opportunities to build relationships with other staff members, a critical component to decreasing the ever present burnout and turnover. By offering on-line collaborative resources and training to staff, Fostering Relationships works toward preventing the staff burnout and turnover that all too often perpetuates the experience of disrupted relationships for the youth.

The Bridges' Transition Framework guides the organization of the cards. Specifically, Fostering Relationships adapted the Bridges' Framework, using four phases of transition: Endings, Uncertainty[1], Beginnings, and Renewal. Specifically, Fostering Relationships included a fourth phase of transition that we refer to as Renewal. Significant trauma, which includes abuse, neglect, and witnessing violence that leads to separations from loved ones, often has an effect on its victims long after the events and conditions have changed. Often, such traumatic experiences are remembered to some degree as though they are being experienced in the present. Even if a person knows rationally that a particular memory is only a memory, he may feel a high level of fear and helplessness corresponding to the original experience. A trigger to the memory can also cause him to react with increased heart rate and breathing, and other body-based reactions of our fight, flight, or freeze responses that trigger when we are threatened. Thus, in trauma there is often a collapsing of time and space, where the past seems subjectively to exist in the present. In this case, it is hard to get distance from the past, and people often feel like they are being overtaken by what has occurred before. Renewal represents the need to heal from trauma, helping the traumatized individual gain a new, holistic perspective on these very troubling earlier experiences. In other words, it means helping them to experience the memory as a memory, and to gain distance from the experience so they can integrate it and make sense of it.

In sum, Fostering Relationships works to support staff as a means to ultimately strength relationships between youth parents and their children, like Susan and Donna, so that they can begin to explore their own internal lives in a way that is relevant, fun, and non-threatening. Pregnant and parenting foster youth are often at a crossroads of a number of different challenges, including the move to late teen and early adult identity formation, and the acquisition of greater capacity as a parent. Any of these challenges requires a lot of energy and work. A combination of them all is likely to be daunting, and all the more so for these people whose past experiences with change have often been traumatizing. By providing some structure around how to engage and think about these changes, Fostering Relationships provides clients with the opportunity to rework older negative experiences, integrate a new sense of self, and to heal their disjointed internal experiences so that they can bring something new to their own children.

NOTE

1. Rather than using the term "Neutral Zone," Fostering Relationships uses "Uncertainty." For many foster youth, "Neutral" does not adequately capture their experience. Major early losses in relationships and other traumas can become very much alive at times of major change. They often color the way a current change is experienced and can make the transition seem overwhelming, creating a time of uncertainty.

REFERENCES

Bowlby, J. (1982). *Attachment and loss: Vol. 1. Attachment*. New York, NY: Basic Books.

Bowlby, J. (1973). *Attachment and loss: Vol. 2. Separation anxiety and anger*. New York, NY: Basic Books.

Bowlby, J. (1988). *A secure base. Clinical applications of attachment theory*. London, England: Routledge.

Bretherton, I., & Munholland, K. A. (2008). Internal working models in attachment relationships: Elaborating a central construct in attachment theory. In J. Cassidy & P. Shaver (Eds.), *Handbook of attachment: Theory, research and clinical application* (2nd ed., pp. 102–130). New York, NY: Guilford.

Cassidy, J. (2008). The nature of the child's ties. In J. Cassidy & P. R. Shaver (Eds.), *Handbook of attachment: Theory, research, and clinical application* (2nd ed., pp. 3–22). New York, NY: Guilford Press.

Chapin Hall. (2006). Foster care youth. The National Campaign to Prevent Teen Pregnancy. Retrieved from http://www.chapinhall.org/sites/default/files/old_reports/315.pdf

Clemmens, D. (2003). Adolescent motherhood: A meta-synthesis of qualitative studies. *The American Journal of Maternal Child Nursing*, *28*, 93–99.

Courtney, M. E., Piliavin, I., Grogan-Kaylor, A., & Nesmith, A. (2001). Foster youth transitions to adulthood: Outcomes 12 to 18 months after leaving out-of-home care. *Child Welfare*, *80*, 685–717.

Dworsky, A., & DeCoursey, J. (2009). *Pregnant and parenting foster youth: Their needs, their experiences*. Chicago, IL: University of Chicago, Chapin Hall Center for Children.

Healthy Teen Network. (2007). Unique needs of children born to teen parents. Retrieved from http://www.healthyteennetwork.org

Herrman, J. W. (2006). The voices of teen mothers: The experience of repeat pregnancy. *The American Journal of Maternal Child Nursing*, *31*, 243–249.

Herrman, J. W. (2007). Repeat pregnancy in adolescence: Intentions and decision making. *The American Journal of Maternal Child Nursing*, *32*, 89–94.

Hermann, J. W. (2010). Assessing the teen parent family: The role for nurses. *Nursing for Women's Health*, *14*, 212–221. doi: 10.1111/j.1751-486X.2010.01542.x

Hoffman, S. (2006). *By the numbers: The public costs of teen childbearing*. Washington, DC: National Campaign to Prevent Teen Pregnancy.

Hoffman S. D., & Maynard R. A. (2008). *Kids having kids: Costs and social consequences of teen pregnancy*. Washington, DC: Urban Institute.

Nittoli, J. (2003). *The unsolved challenge of system reform: The condition of the frontline human services workforce*. Baltimore, MD: The Annie E. Casey Foundation.

O'Hare, W. P. (2001). *A KIDS COUNT/PRB report on census 2000*. Baltimore MD: The Annie E. Casey Foundation.

Pecora, P. J., Kessler, R. C., Williams, J., O'Brien, K., Downs, C. A., & English, D. (2005). Improving family foster care: Findings from the northwest foster care alumni study. Seattle, WA: Casey Family Programs. Retrieved from http://www.casey.org/resources/publications/pdf/improvingfamilyfostercare_es.pdf

Savio Beers, L. A., & Hollo, R. E. (2009). Approaching the adolescent-headed family: a review of teen parenting. *Current Problems in Pediatric and Adolescent Health Care, 39*, 216–233.

Van Ryzin, M. J., Mills, D., Kelban, S., Vars, M. R., & Chamberlain, P. (2011). Using the Bridges Transition Framework for youth in foster care: Measurement development and preliminary outcomes. *Children & Youth Services Review, 33*, 2267–2272.

Weir, K. N., Fife, S. T., Whiting, J. B., & Blazewick, A. (2008). Clinical training of MFTs for adoption, foster care, and child development settings: A comparative survey of CACREP, COAMFTE, and CSWE accredited programs. *Journal of Family Psychotherapy, 19*, 277–290. doi: 10.1080/08975350802269517

Index

For Product Safety Concerns and Information please contact our
EU representative GPSR@taylorandfrancis.com Taylor & Francis
Verlag GmbH, Kaufingerstraße 24, 80331 München, Germany